Are We Making Good Men Better?

A Quest For Knowledge and Spiritual Growth

Jorge L. Aladro, P.G.M.

First Printing
Melbourne, Florida
Blue Note Publications, Inc.

ISBN No.: 978-0-9963066-3-8
Library of Congress Catalog Number: 2015940896

Cover Design: Carmen Abreu

Printed In The United States of America

This work is dedicated to those who seek light in their quest for knowledge and understanding of the necessities needed to maintain inviolate the spirit and principles of the Mystic Art.

LUX FIAT ET LUX FIT

Dedication

This book is dedicated to those Brothers that believe in and live Masonry on a daily basis. You are the generation of observant Masons that will secure and convey Freemasonry pure and unimpaired to our latest posterity. Thank you for your dedication, commitment and sacrifice for this Noble, Ancient and Honorable Institution. Stay true, focused and perseverant. Our task is too important to leave it to chance.

Acknowledgements

No one individual stands alone in any of his or her accomplishments and I'm certainly no different. To my wife Bonnie and family I'm so grateful for all their love and support in all my endeavors and my heart felt gratitude to my dear friend and Brother M∴W∴ J. Dick Martinez who has assisted me in proof reading my documents and for always being there when I call.

Contents

PREFACE

I hope and pray this book has found its way into your library because you are a lover of the Fraternity, because you are concerned for it and are looking for ways to make yourself and the Fraternity better.

Up front and for the benefit of disclosure you will not find anything in this book that is politically correct, as I do not believe that political correctness has a place in Freemasonry, regardless of its place in society. Freemasonry must always be presented in a truthful and forthright manner.

I congratulate you on your enthusiasm for the Fraternity. Here you will find an honest observation of the Craft as I see it, based on my Masonic experiences of nearly forty years working in the quarries of something I hold very near and dear to my soul.

Nearly forty years of Masonry that started my career unbeknownst to me in a clandestine Lodge, which practiced the Scottish Rite Obedience, and where for a young man of twenty-one years I was very involved in the operations of the Lodge and the parent body. There I learned many lessons about Masonry and life until sometime later when I discovered the difference between Regular and Clandestine Freemasonry.

Joining regular Freemasonry I applied myself just as hard because of the love for the Craft and what it meant to me. In my home Lodge I found many great Masons that looked out for my welfare and became Mentors not only by words but also by deeds.

I advanced through my Symbolic Lodge and became Worshipful Master. Because of my previous error in joining a clandestine Lodge, Masonic Education became even more important to me and I wanted to learn as much as possible about the Craft and apply those lessons in my life and work. I wanted to live a Masonic Way of life and share that knowledge with my Lodge Brothers.

The good Lord has been kind to me and allowed me to reach other offices within the Fraternity when I thought it would not be possible. For several reasons I was outspoken, and more importantly I was not a sycophant, and even with my limitations I was able to reach the office of Grand Master in 2012.

I took a good long look at the fraternal side of Freemasonry, which very few do and what I found was not pretty. This has laid heavy on my mind and has made me follow a course where I needed to share this information with those likeminded Masons in our Fraternity, hoping that as a result of it we can bring a renewed interest and awareness to our Fraternity that we may be able to influence it for the better.

There are many Masonic authors that have written countless volumes about the Craft mysteries, rituals, symbolism, history, philosophy, etc., but not many will speak to you about the state of the Craft and this book addresses some of the areas which raised grave concern to me.

I was concerned enough to write this small book to

address them in what I think will shed some light on the things that matter to our Fraternity for its survival.

During my tenure as a Grand Lodge Officer I wrote many short Masonic Discourses addressing numerous Masonic subjects in an effort to educate and exchange ideas with the Craft. I wanted to challenge them to think the "what if's," we did the right things by the Fraternity in every aspect of it from design to concept so the world would know us not for our charities, but for the content of our character.

As Masons we should be free thinkers, and in order to fulfill this requirement we must have knowledge of that which Freemasonry is supposed to be and we can only obtain that knowledge from reading and research. We need to become well acquainted with our Constitutions, Rules and Regulations so that we may observe them as they were intended and make sure others follow them as well, as we swore to in our different obligations and charges as members of this Fraternity.

If Masonry is our profession then we must practice the Mystic Art in and out of our Lodges and be examples for our Brethren from the way we dress to the way we behave. We must have the knowledge and impart that knowledge to those less informed, as well as sharing it with all our Brothers that we may elevate Freemasonry not only for our members but also for the benefit of mankind.

If we are going to "Make Good Men Better" one man at a time we must first place our house in order and I believe this book will help you do just that. Our task is too important. The results are vital, not only for our survival but to also fulfill our goal of making good men better for the benefit of mankind.

Freemasonry is for us to save or lose. I hope this book can

assist you in seeing the difference between where we are and where we need to be. The future is ours. I pray we can be able to stand tall and proclaim victory with a resounding YES to the question: Are We Making Good Men Better?

In conclusion, I hope this book opens new horizons and guides your footsteps in search of further light in Masonry, and that it sparks the flame in your lantern of knowledge to burn ever brighter for your lifetime commitment of seeking truth and knowledge.

MINERVA
Goddess Of Wisdom

Chapter 1

Are We Making Good Men Better?

"Think like a man of action, act like man of thought."
—Henri Bergson

"To improve myself in Masonry!" My Brothers, this is what this book is all about. Since the advent of several movies and numerous documentaries we have experienced a renaissance in Freemasonry. Although many of these are not negative of Masonry, their description of Masonry leaves a little to be desired, thus creating a craving for curiosity that can be counterproductive to this Ancient Craft.

Over the nearly three centuries of Modern day existence Masonry has had many who have come to us as curiosity seekers. Many of them have stayed but never seen in Masonry its beauty and light. This of course is not a new phenomenon. It has happened many times before and it will continue to happen in the future. However, we can make a difference. How you ask? The same way we have always done it before, by answering the question: What came you here to do?

First and foremost you must be honest in your answer to the question. Did you come to satisfy your curiosity, were you looking for a service organization, were you looking to belong to a social club, or were you looking to belong to a good ol' boys club? If you were, you may find a Lodge that will deliver just that, however Masonry is so much more. Masonry is the world's premier self-improvement society.

It was the very first society that created a group of men with sufficient knowledge to rival that of the clergy and feudal lords. The Operative Masons were the first group to impart knowledge in the art of building magnificent structures throughout Europe to those who qualified to become members. These men entered into a compact with others to preserve the Mystic Art of building great things. They were Entered Apprentices for seven years, before reaching the status of Fellow of the Craft.

During this period of time the Entered Apprentice had to demonstrate his ability to learn and improve himself in the art of building. These time-tested structures are still in use several centuries later. They built the structures in order to stand the test of time under the watchful supervision of the Fellows of the Craft and Master Overseers.

Those who could not create a masters piece could not become a Fellow of the Craft. Promotion was only given by merit, after due and proper examination of their work. That is the reason those buildings stand today. They only accepted the very best craftsmen.

Now we move forward into the era of Speculative Masons and we find that in the transition from Operative to Speculative Masonry we start to erode the principles of discipline, value and honor of its long tradition and history. Hence as a result came the birth of the Grand Lodge in an effort to maintain the core value of the institution, and the birth of Modern Masonry as we know it today.

So if you came here looking for a service organization, social club or good ol' boys club this manuscript is not for you. You will not find herein anything that contributes to that effort or endeavor for this is not the purpose of this book. As a matter of fact, it is quite the contrary. If you know what came you here to do? Welcome aboard and enjoy the journey. A journey that will carry you through a lifetime of personal and spiritual growth the like you have never seen if you properly apply the lessons and study the hidden meaning of the Mystic Art.

Masonry is a way of life, a school where the graduation is in that house not made with hands eternal in the heavens. Your graduation ceremony starts with those immortal words "well done good and faithful fellow."

You see my Brother, Masonry is certainly not found in a One Day Class, as this is contrary to everything taught in Masonry. Masonry's initiatic process is different for everyone. It is not just about the process it is about the individual experience and how the Brother will accept and adopt that process into his own life.

This initiatic process will be lost in a fast trip where you are not a participant as this is as much a part of the Degree and experience necessary. That is why your senses of hearing, smelling and feeling are first exposed to the process before your eyes can behold the beauty of the sacred space you had just entered.

You were first prepared to be a Mason in your heart as this was your desire to join of your own free will and accord. You came seeking something that your heart desired before you were able to see it. This is purposely done to awaken your senses and let your imagination absorb all the sounds carried to you by interactive tongues and grab your soul as you go into a life-altering experience.

If you do not accept the lessons of the initiatic process you will never dwell in the depth of the lessons taught in it. No parts of the Degrees are frivolous as they teach essential lessons of self-improvement both personal and spiritually and they are contained not only in the ritual but in the great light of Masonry "God's Holy Word."

The mere thought of a One Day Class places this Meritorious, Worthy and Distinguished Fraternal Order on the same par as a college fraternity; prank initiations without meaning and void of any lessons except those of excess and intemperance. This could not be further from what the Fraternity has stood for centuries.

We must stand steadfast on this principle; anything that takes away from the very initiatic process is contrary to Freemasonry. Anything that takes away from selecting the very best from society, robs this Fraternal Order from its intended origin, where only the best was chosen to be a Fellow of the Craft.

So if you came here to improve yourself in Masonry I firmly believe that you will benefit from the words written in this manuscript as we attempt to address those things that would outline both personal and spiritual growth.

We will address both the inner and outer qualities of a Mason, his conduct in and out of the Lodge, as well as the progress of improving himself and the effectual changes while progressing through the Degrees and a journey of a lifetime towards that undiscovered country that house not made with hands eternal in the heavens.

While on this journey it will be ever important that you

commit to self-evaluations often, measured against the raw individual that once seek the LIGHT OF MASONRY, and mark well those changes. Your measure of improvement will be the difference in the man before and after the initiation and will maintain over the course of a lifetime of personal and spiritual evolution of oneself.

Only you will be the judge of your inner and outer evolution. However, those who are your Brothers, Friends, and Family will be able to measure that metamorphosis by the changes in the inner and outer demeanor of your conduct.

Only those that find improvement in the course of a lifetime will find the true secrets of Freemasonry. As for the others they will always find the true secrets to be elusive if they are not properly prepared in their hearts and minds and only believe that Masonry is nothing more than a social club.

So here we are at another crossroads just like the ones we met and overcame many times in the nearly three centuries of our modern existence, starting in 1717. Later came the Ancient movement, the Morgan Affair, the Anti-Masonic Party, the Depression, and post WWII baby boomers, among others.

These events served to create different challenges to our Institution. In every instance we had to draw back concentrating on the basics shoring up our beliefs and solidifying our resolve in the well-grounded principles and morals of our Institution, this reaction to the events brought us back to our former glory. As humans we continue to stumble over the same obstacles. The further we move from any tragic event the more we turn away from the very things that made us great.

Here you will find what you came here to do. I pray this

book will challenge you to think, inspire you to read, to research, and to discuss those things which will open new doors to your understandings. Improve and challenge yourself to performing nobler deeds and greater achievements. This will guide you on your way to achieving a Masonic Way of Life.

At the same time you will be setting higher standards for yourself, Lodge, and Fraternity in your corner of the world. Be a leader—make it happen.

Chapter 2

Improving Yourself In Masonry

"As we continue to improve ourselves in Masonry,
we are indeed improving life."
—*Stanley F. Maxwell*

Improving yourself in Masonry will involve many phases, which will require many changes in your personal and spiritual lifestyle in order for the man to go through the metamorphosis that will eventually evolve into a practicing Mason.

Some of the life-altering changes will be easy to recognize by any Brother that has received and understands the lessons in the Three Degrees of Freemasonry such as speech, dress, and manner of conduct in Lodge and in public.

Masonry places many limitations, starting with who can be a Member and what the Members can do or not do within the Lodge or outside the Lodge regardless of what the norm is in the society in which you live.

Freedom of speech is the balance by what is proper or not proper to be discussed. The manner in which it can be discussed is something you should have known before you became a Mason by reading the by-laws of the Lodge that you are petitioning. When in Lodge it is limited by the bounds, which have been accepted by Masons since time immemorial. When outside of the Lodge you must be obedient to the civil laws that dictate its use. However, if in expressing yourself you find it necessary to portray yourself as a Mason, wearing Masonic rings, shirts etc., you must temper your speech as not to discredit Freemasonry.

First, speech while in an assembled Lodge is a very important part of our work and understanding as to how a Lodge must operate in order to maintain civility and order.

While in Lodge no one should be discussing politics or religion, this has always been strictly forbidden.

No one shall speak in open Lodge without having permission from the Worshipful Master, and proper decorum is to rise unto your feet and wait to be recognized by the Master before speaking.

No one shall have separate conversation while in open Lodge without permission of the Master. You are not to talk of anything impertinent or unseemly, nor interrupt the Master, Wardens, or Brother speaking to the Master, nor use any language unbecoming a Mason under any pretense.

No one shall say anything offensive that may prevent easy and free conversation because this will destroy our harmony and defeat our laudable purposes.

A Mason must always be courteous in conversation with other Brothers within and without the Lodge in never using vulgar language

A Mason must always be cautious when speaking around

strangers so that no secrets will be exposed and that the reputation of the Fraternity may be placed in doubt for the manner in which you are speaking.

Proper conversation elevates the minds and the souls and it is the principle means of communication between Brothers. One of the ways we as Masons need to improve ourselves is in being able to communicate by word our feelings, ideas and principles. There is no doubt Masonry will help us develop our public speaking and provide us a platform to carry on discussions with civility and honor.

Proper attire is another way that Masonry elevates men of all walks of life. Proper attire speaks volumes of who the individual is or may be. Knowing how to dress properly for all occasions is a very important part of life. It demonstrates the importance you have given to whatever occasions you may be participating.

The way you dress will set your first impression upon all those you meet. The way you dress and carry yourself in public or Masonic Lodge, will establish the way people think about you long before they have had an opportunity to meet you.

It may be that your Lodge has a dress code for Officers as well as Members, and you too should be a part of this ritual of dressing up as an Officer or Member.

In most Lodges around the world proper attire to attend a Lodge at minimum will be a dark suit and a dark tie. This can be observed in most European Lodges and other Lodges around the world.

Other Lodges may have the accepted traditional dress of the country in which they reside which will be the equivalent to a dark suit, not in the dress manner but in the significance of that type of clothing. The importance of a dress code pays homage to the Fraternity and displays its significance in our order.

Some may say and I have heard that Masonry focuses on the internal and not the external qualifications of a man, and that dress does not matter. This could not be further from the truth.

First, Masonry elevates the entire man, not just parts of him. The manner in which the man dresses is part of his transformation and the Masonic experience.

Secondly, to think or to say that if one Brother cannot meet this minimum of requirements, it is putting that Brother down as if he is somewhat of a lesser Mason than the rest (those who can meet what is expected of them) couldn't be further from the truth. If that is the case there are many ways to assist the Brother. However, if the reason for this behavior is the fact the Brother refuses to improve his appearance because he misunderstands our Masonic Society and is confusing it with an old boys club instead of the Premier self-improvement society this Fraternity is just not for him.

You will find this to be a breakdown of the Recommenders and Investigation Committee that failed to recognize this individual as a non-conformist to whom Masonry was not properly explained. Our Fraternity has an overwhelming number of these Brothers who tend to bring down the decorum and high standards of our Institution for whatever reason or excuse they may have.

On the other hand, if Masonry is this important to him that he dresses up a couple times a month to spend time with his Brothers in this sacred sanctuary we call a Masonic Lodge he is indeed worthy of praise and emulation. This shows how much Masonry means to him and his high regard for our Fraternity.

This has been a gentlemen's organization since its inception and should be maintained like that for our posterity. Nothing short of that should be accepted.

One only has to look at the pictures of old to see our Brothers dressed appropriately for Lodge and Grand Lodge occasions even if they only had one suit, thus showing their respect for the Institution.

Your behavior while in the Lodge must be so that you do not disturb the harmony of the Lodge. Participate with your Brothers in promoting an atmosphere of warmth and peace where the Brothers can dwell together in unity.

Remember the following Ancient Charges as to your behavior among Brothers, strangers and family and keep them ever present in your minds so as not to discredit this Honorable Institution.

Your behavior before or after Lodge is over, where you may enjoy yourselves with innocent mirth, treating one another with proper respect in your friendship, avoiding all excess or forcing anyone to indulge in anything beyond his inclination or keeping him from going when he needs to leave, must always be present on your mind.

You are never to bring to the Lodge any private piques or quarrels, much less problems about religion or politics which have never been discussed in Lodge and never will be as to protect the sanctity of the Lodge and maintain harmony within its peaceable walls.

Your behavior when meeting a Brother out and about in the world where no strangers are present requires you to salute one another in a courteous manner, calling each other Brother without intruding upon each other, which may take away any respect that may be due a Brother. All Masons are thought of as Brothers on the same level.

Yet, we must be cognizant that some Brothers may have earned certain honors, which will add to and not take away from his character as a revered individual within the community. This should be recognized as such when appropriate to avoid ill manners.

Your behavior as a Mason among non-Masons must be so that nothing that is not proper to discuss with them is discussed or reveal anything about Masonry that may lead them to discover or find out what is improper for them to know. It may be necessary that you do not enter into such discussions. This is to be done prudently and courteously to protect the honor and reputation of the Fraternity.

Your behavior at home and in your neighborhood must be becoming a moral and wise man. Do not let your family, friends, and neighbors know the concerns of the Lodge that are not to be discussed outside of the Lodge so that you may protect the honor and reputation of this Honorable Institution.

You must also remember that the character of the Fraternity rests upon your shoulders. Therefore you must not be out too late or too long from home after Lodge hours are past. Avoid gluttony or drunkenness so that your family will not be neglected or injured, nor you disabled from working. Remember the reputation of the Fraternity is depending on your good behavior.

Your behavior towards an individual claiming to be a Brother must be cautious so as to examine him in such a way as carefully as possible. In that way you give no secrets away and can reject the impostor.

However, if you discover him to be a Brother, you are to respect him accordingly. If you find him to be in need, you are to assist him if you can or direct him on how he can be assisted.

You ought to at all times avoid all bickering, arguing, slurs and backbiting, Do not permit others to slander any honest Brother, but defend his character and do right by him.

If you are wronged by a Brother you must apply to your Lodge or his and from there to Grand Lodge if necessary; seeking effectual remedy as our predecessors have done before. Never take a legal course unless the case cannot be otherwise decided. Patiently listen to the honest and friendly advice of the Master and Brethren when they stop you from going to the law who are strangers to our Fraternity, and would request of you to end all law-suits, that you may be more cognizant that Masonic matters are dealt with better within the Fraternity. The Master and Brethren should kindly offer their mediation, which ought to be thankfully submitted to by the contending Brothers. If this submission is impossible, they must however carry their process or lawsuit without anger and bitterness, saying or doing nothing which may hinder Brotherly Love and beneficial acts to be continued so that everyone can see the gentle influence of Masonry, as all true Masons have done from time immemorial.

As a Mason you must speak, dress, and act the part. You are now someone's impression of a Mason and must convey yourself as such at all times.

Some of the leadership are in such a hurry to make Masons that they deliver the wrong message to those exalted to the Sublime Degree of Master Masons that we will take you anyway and anywhere, lowering our standards and requirements. What we must remember is that if they do not have the time to dedicate to Masonry by receiving the Degrees in the usual manner, they will not have the time to dedicate to Masonry period.

By bringing a Candidate that does not have the time to

learn and participate in the Craft, we run the risk of them not understanding the mission of Masonry. Eventually he becomes disenfranchised from the lack of understanding since he has not participated, been mentored or taught anything but what he could absorb in one long day when he received the Degrees, sacrificing the Masonic experience for expediency. This will lead to no participation, and eventually a Brother who will stop paying his dues because he has not received any benefits from the Craft. Who knows, he may even become a Masonic detractor because of his lack of understanding.

Do not let anyone tell you that you cannot be the very best you can be. Do not let anyone tell you that you are ok the way you are. You came here to improve on what you already had and only you can do that for yourself. If personal and spiritual growth is your goal this will require a lifetime of dedication to reach these goals. You can do it and your Brothers will be there for you every step of the way.

I don't believe anyone looking to be a Mason is looking for less than the Masonic experience and as such you will be cheated out of all the other little things that come with the traditional raising. The relationship you will develop with the Instructors and Mentors as well as members of your class when is composed of five or less candidates could never be found in a One Day Class.

Masonry is not for everyone. If you are looking for the hidden treasures of Masonry, they do not come in gold and diamond. The hidden treasures of Masonry come within each one of us and are different for everyone. They will be found in the path by which each one of us reach our personal and spiritual growth and become better men and Masons.

Regardless of whether you are a one-day Mason or not,

you deserve better, and you need to elevate yourself in the Fraternity by following its tenants, principles, and customs. You need to improve yourself in Masonry by the way you speak, dress, and conduct yourself, and only then can you master your personal and spiritual building efforts.

Chapter 3

Are They Worthy and Well Qualified?

"The measure of a man's character is what he would do if he would never be found out."
—*Thomas Macaulay*

Although some may think that all the recent publicity is good for Masonry, I beg to differ. What this has brought us are more curiosity seekers and naysayers wanting to see what we are truly about which perhaps they may never understand.

For one, I'm not concerned with the numbers. What concerns me the most is the quality of the men seeking light in Masonry. Masonry makes good men better. We do not make bad men good. Masonry is not, has never been, nor will be in the future a place for rehabilitation of men. This we leave to society and the authorities to make that call. We are only interested in the pure at heart that want to be better, who are looking to explore the lessons taught in our mysteries. He tries to achieve perfection even when he knows it is impossible because man on earth is in the pursuit of excellence to imitate his Creator, the Great Architect of the Universe, even though he knows it is not achievable.

Now these new candidates may have come to you from unknown sources. There is nothing wrong with this scenario, as long as you remember that if you don't know them, you must NOT recommend them. Just as you would not recommend a stranger to your boss, or vouched for an individual you do not know as a character witness in a court of law, serve as an alibi to a total stranger or co-sign a loan to an unknown person

You must know the material you are recommending to your Lodge. Remember this individual will be our future Brother and you and your family will be exposed to him and the peace of your Lodge as well as the safety of your love ones may be at stake.

The best way to get to know this individual is to interact with him and his family. There is nothing wrong with inviting him or them to participate in Lodge dinners and spend time with members to get to know him and his family before we present them with a petition. There is no rush. If he is truly a seeker of knowledge he will understand why we must take our time to weed out those not qualified. Remember our slogan of "making good men better."

There are many Lodges that use these practices and have great success in obtaining new and quality material, and they have not been in a rush to get them a petition. Some of the candidates have waited as long as six months while participating in all the functions of the Lodge. These include attending all meetings for the fellowship before the Lodge opened, and dinners, if any are served. These Lodges have programs of Masonic Education or information for the public that they can attend. This type of information can lead to the individual inquiring to change his mind or reaffirm his conviction of becoming a Mason.

Another tool being used to keep curiosity seekers away are the fees charged for the Degrees. Most of the Lodges that have great success in attracting serious candidates have a high price for the Degrees, more especially the Entered Apprentice. This has been a good tool in weeding themselves out, as their inquisitiveness proves to be weaker than the power of the dollar.

There is nothing in Masonry that requires anyone to sign the petition of a Candidate who they do not know, yet it is done every day in America. I hope that there are no rewards for a Brother to be top line signer or second line signer as the decision to be a Mason should never be influenced by someone who is looking for a merit reward. Influencing a possible Candidate to make such an important decision is a possible violation in many jurisdictions.

When you read the history of Freemasonry you never hear of the number of Masons unless you are especially looking for the census information. However, you always hear of the quality of the members that adorned our Fraternity. We are very proud to site names from all over the world of the "who's who," if you will.

Masonry was never intended for the masses; Masonry has always been for the finest and yet has never been a snobbish organization, as our principles and tenets teach us to behave otherwise.

We have always accepted men from all walks of life, from all professions and vocations, as long as they are good men seeking further light in their lives and willing to improve themselves by becoming a better participant in their place of worship, a better citizen, father, son, husband, and neighbor.

As our Ritual states, if Masonry is said to have a weak point it is when we take in a new member. So there are many lessons to learn while we adhere to this warning by our predecessors who deemed this of such great importance that it was incorporated into our Ritual as a warning not to let our guard down.

Here is how we can perform our duties and be fair to both, the applicant and the Fraternity. First and foremost is by performing our investigations using the same guidelines each and every time in the most stringent manner and with no deviation under any circumstances.

Follow your jurisdiction's regulations and go the extra step to assure yourselves that only quality material will be made available for Initiation.

Here are some recommendations that will benefit both the Lodge and the Candidate.

Start by eliminating the need or thought that we must make Masons indiscriminately to reach quantities of an elusive past of wrong doing when quality was ignored and Masons were rushed through Degree mills with little or no mentoring or education except a limited catechism.

Our very own beginnings came about to defeat or eliminate this very line of thinking by self-imposing higher standards, which would be enforced by a higher authority created exactly for this purpose. This was the idea of a Grand Lodge concentrating on quality and rejecting indiscriminate quantity.

Unthinkable as it may be, today the Grand Lodges are primarily responsible for this artificial necessity to increase membership for they see this as a way to maintain the organization forgetting the principles that created them. This may lead to its very own demise from the undesirables being brought in by bias recommendations and poor investigations designed to increase membership at whatever cost.

Do not get me wrong we want new blood. To say otherwise would be irresponsible and the signing of the death certificate of the Order.

What I am saying here is that we need quality not quantity. Therefore, we need to adopt the army's slogan, which says "We are looking for a few good men." We are not looking nor do we want just anyone. We want the best of the best.

Slow the process and rush from the signing of petition to the raising; making sure the recommenders, committees, instructors and mentors truly understand that there is no need to rush. Express the need to be thorough in their work as we are dealing with a complex being. They need all our attention, understanding and assistance to succeed.

On the other hand, when in doubt do not be afraid to vote in favor of the Fraternity. Today we place too much negativity on an appropriate rejection of an unqualified candidate. We have placed so much emphasis on recruiting that we have reached the mentality that a rejection is a sin or deathblow to the Fraternity when in fact it may be completely the opposite. It may save the peace and tranquility of the Lodge.

Again, when it comes to making a choice always err on the side of the Craft, having said that, if you use the awesome power of the vote as a personal vendetta against a recommender, for personal reasons against the petitioner, or because you have an axe to grind against the Lodge then you must take another look at the man in the mirror. It is obvious you have missed some very important lessons in Masonry and will have to answer to your Maker for your hypocrisy, hatred and wrong doing, not to mention the fact that you have dishonored yourself by such hideous action.

We need to look at everything and ask any questions deemed necessary now before the applicant is accepted. Remember you are the sentinel of the wellbeing of our Fraternity. On your shoulders rests our reputation, peace and tranquility of our Lodge. You have an awesome responsibility to make sure you ask for help if you have any doubts. It is better now than after the applicant is initiated. Do not get complacent with your duties and remember this is our weakest point. Guard well The West Gate.

In closing this chapter I leave you with the following quote from one of the most prolific Masonic writers of his time Reverend and Brother George Oliver, D.D. (1782-1867), who said it best when writing this charge to the Craft and I quote, "Be very cautious whom you recommend as a Candidate for Initiation: one false step on this part may be fatal. If you introduce a disputatious (argumentative) person, confusion will be produced, which may end in the dissolution of the Lodge, you have a good Lodge, keep it select. Great Numbers are not always beneficial."

Chapter 4

Petitioners and Recommenders

*"Courage is the first of human qualities, because
it is the quality which guarantees all the others."*
— *Winston Churchill*

Have you ever cosigned a loan for someone you do not
know or recently met like in the last few minutes or
days? I bet NOT, and the reason is not because your name
would be libel, but because you would be monetarily liable
for the indebtedness.

Well Masonry does not hold you monetarily responsible
when you sign your name to a petition as a cosigner, however
it hopes that you would know the person before you commit
yourself to signing such a petition otherwise you may slander
your name when he defaults on his obligations.

You wonder why? Simply you just recommended and gave
your word to the Brethren of your Lodge that this individual
was quality material to join Masonry.

In other countries the recommenders are held responsible for the character of the petitioner they avouched for by cosigning the petition or solicitation for membership. I wish we were like that in our Grand Jurisdictions.

In comparison, the average petition from the Grand Lodges in the States will ask the Recommenders to sign the petition under the following statement: "We recommend the above petitioner as a candidate for the Degrees of Masonry based upon our belief that he is of good moral character, temperate, industrious."

As a contrast, let me share with you what the United Grand Lodge of England, Mother Grand Lodge of the World requires of their Recommenders or as they call them the Proposer and Seconder in the petition for the Degrees of Masonry.

The following questions are asked from both the Proposer (top line signer) and the Seconder (second line signer) followed by a declaration where they must, under signature, attest to their knowledge of the Candidate and the validity of his statements as well as their responses.

1. How long have you known the Candidate?

2. To the best of your knowledge and belief are his answers to question 5 on the Registration Form true?

Question 5 of the Candidates section.

a) I have never been convicted by a court of any offence.

b) I have never been the subject of a finding of dishonest or disgraceful conduct.

c) I have never been disciplined by any professional, trade or other tribunal.

d) I am not awaiting the outcome of proceedings against

me before a criminal court or a professional, trade or other tribunal.

e) I am not to the best of my knowledge the subject of any criminal, professional, trade or other investigation.

3. Do you meet him often?

4. Where do you meet him?

a) In your home?

b) In his home?

c) At work?

d) Socially?

e) Elsewhere (give details)?

5. Would you welcome him into your home?

6. Do you vouch for him in every respect as a suitable and desirable person for admission to the Craft?

7. a) Would his home or business circumstances make it difficult for him to attend regularly at Lodge meetings?

b) Do you accept the responsibility of encouraging him to make his membership effective?

8. Have you informed him of:

a) His financial obligations to the Lodge and

b) The calls that may be made on his time?

9 What reason have you for thinking Freemasonry will interest him? (This last question has space below it for hand written answer from both recommenders.)

Certification of the Proposer, Seconder among others needed to qualify the Candidate are as follows:

I, the Proposer, declares as follows:-
The Candidate has been personally known to me for

_____years _____months.

To the best of my knowledge, information and belief the statements made by the Candidate on this application form are true and correct: he is a man of good reputation and well fitted to become a member of this Lodge.

[For candidates for Initiation only] The answer given me to the questions above are true.

Dated this_____ day of_____20_____
Name of Proposer/Seconder_____

Chapter 5

Investigators Or Rubber Stampers

"Guard well the West Gate"
—Unknown

Guarding the West Gate is probably the single most important thing we can do when so many curiosity seekers, pretenders and deceivers are looking into Masonry.

Personally I'm still not certain whether all the publicity through the fictional best sellers and movies has done the Fraternity any good. Some may say that good or bad, publicity is still publicity; however, I think it has not all been for the best.

The way the Fraternity has been portrayed full of mysteries and hidden treasures rather than its principles and tenets; the emphasis on countless interpretations of the symbols; the connections with the occult and alchemy, none of which would be found in probably 98% of the Lodges, may lead the Candidate to be disappointed in what he finds.

I'm of the firm belief that Freemasonry should be

promoted and lived up to for what has been its main slogan —"Making Good Men Better." I consider Freemasonry to be the Premier Self-improvement Society, in the operative and speculative sense.

So the kind of material we are looking to work with has not changed with very minor exceptions. We are still looking for good men that want to make themselves better.

- We are NOT a rehabilitation center for men with bad habits or poor behavior.
- We are NOT a training school for low self-esteem.
- We are NOT looking for the selfish.
- We are NOT seeking the contentious.
- We are NOT searching for the nonconformist.
- We are NOT recruiting the crude, rough, and cruel.
- We are NOT pursuing the devious and deceitful.
- We are NOT considering the atheist.

The quality of the membership rests on the recommenders as we have previously discussed in the first case and on those that are in charge of the investigations as the second line of defense.

Whether your Grand Lodge conducts national background investigations or not, it is imperative that the Investigation Committee perform its duties flawlessly. The very future of our Fraternity and the quality of the membership rests on their shoulders.

Visiting and having individual personal contact with the petitioner while his family is present during the course of the investigation is of the highest importance. This may give you an insight into the type of man he is and how he can provide for his family, or if it creates an additional burden on his family.

Is the family in agreement with the petitioner or do they have reservations? Will they be supportive of him or not? This can make a great difference in the participation of the Candidate.

Can he afford all of the expenses and the prompt payment of them? Ask the spouse about the financial indebtedness he will be incurring by joining and the prompt payment expected of his annual dues.

Does their financial situation allow them to practice charity on a regular basis in order to help, aid and assist the needy, the hungry and the destitute?

Are they religious people and do they practice their faith? Do they meet the requirements of your Grand Lodge? Although we are not a religion we do have certain requirements for our candidates to meet.

Is his or the spouses religion in opposition to Masonry which can cause the Candidate an additional burden which ultimately may cause him to withdraw from Masonry.

Does he belong to other groups such as social, religious, political, sports and/or hobbies? Does he participate in them and how much time can he dedicate to Masonry? Is he over stretched, and will it be better if he waits until he can find the time necessary for his learning and expanding on his Masonic career?

Have you talked to his neighbors to see if he is a good neighbor? Does he keep his home in the same manner or better than the rest of the neighborhood? Have the police been called to the house? Is he loud and obnoxious, rude and crude? How does he behave with his neighbors? Is he active in his neighborhood?

Have you contacted his references? Has he provided good information on his references? Have you seen if the time known matches? Where do they know him from, and what can they tell you about him? In their opinion will he be a good fit with Masonry? Do they have any knowledge of trouble with law enforcement officers? Ask them about his character, life style and habits. Is he a hard worker, charitable, caring, a good husband, father, son, etc?

Have you talked to his boss if he has one? If not have you talked to his employees? Is he a considerate employer/employee? Does he work well with others? Is he opinionated? Does he work hard to be the best at what he does? Does his work allow him enough free time to participate in Freemasonry? Is he punctual in the performance of his duties? Will he be given a good reference if he were to leave work? Would he be rehired if he came back?

Have you looked on the web under his name? Have you checked his Facebook, Myspace, LinkedIn, YouTube or other social media outlets? His posts may say much about the individual. Is he civil, well-mannered and refined in his conduct and expression? If he is not, this may speak volumes of the individual. We already have too many trouble Brothers that abuse their membership in Masonry by proclaiming to be Masons while conducting themselves as rogue and vulgar individuals in social media outlets, using profane language and making religious and political commentary contrary to what is acceptable in Freemasonry.

Have you talked to the recommenders? Do they really know the man? Interview them about all the things previously discussed; religion, family, neighbors, references, work, hobbies, etc. before you speak to anyone else and compared your notes with what you find out and determined if the recommender knows the candidate or not. If he doesn't know him, this should raise many questions as he is guaranteeing by signing his name on the petition that this individual is Masonic material. This may be a great opportunity to teach the recommenders of their duties and responsibilities to the Brethren, Lodge and future Candidate.

Remember, as the ritual says that if there was to be a weak side to Freemasonry it is that when a candidate petitions our Fraternity. Here is our biggest danger and yet we have Brothers that trample over one another to sign a petition for someone they don't even know.

The Investigation Committee needs to understand the awesome responsibility to the Craft to make sure that they recommend only individuals of the highest character. Anything less will bring discredit to them personally, regardless of the fact that they may have been picked because they have not performed well in the past and recommend anything that comes before them for the sake of filling our ranks.

There has been much written on the importance of this committee and how it should be conducted, of their responsibilities to the Candidate, the Lodge, and the Institution.

Many of these publications can be found in your Constitutions, Rules and Regulations on Masonic Education Booklets and Courses, Masonic Leadership, in your Grand Lodge, other Grand Lodges or the Masonic Services Association (MSA) for free download.

There can be no doubt of the importance of the Investigation Committee, however, if there is any doubt whatsoever as to the individual being recommended one should always rule in favor of the Institution. There is too much at stake to do otherwise and the very reputation of the Freemasonry may rest on it.

Chapter 6

Deceivers, Frauds & Cheats

*"Knowing what's right doesn't mean much
unless you do what's right."*
—*Teddy Roosevelt*

During my tenure as a leader in my state I was absolutely stunned by the way a great number of Brethren were very comfortable with overlooking wrongdoing and reprehensible behavior. I was totally shocked at the amount of defenders the wrongdoers had, willing to ignore the requirements of moral rectitude required by Masonry of Masons and how willing and happy they all were to hide or ignore the facts before them.

It is astonishing that the closer you get to the top the more you get exposed to the ugly side of the Fraternity and you can do two things—one is to ignore it and send it down to be handled or not at the local level and not be bothered, or do something about it by which you may become somewhat unpopular for doing the right thing. That is what you swore to in your many obligations you have taken on the way to the top.

A Mason in all sense of the word is a man of unquestionable righteousness, morality, and rectitude of conduct; bound by his word which he gave at the time of his respective obligations before his fellow Masons and most importantly his God. Our obligations are binding, serious, and honorable.

To do anything different must reflect as a stain on the character of the individual that committed such a violation before God and man, failing in his charge to keep the reputation of the Fraternity unsullied.

These actions are so reprehensible that he should receive the disgrace, shame, and humiliation of every member of the Fraternity or at least from those that believe in their obligations and hold their word to be their bond between themselves, mankind, and their Creator.

There can be no doubt that we have many among us that have taken the various obligations but look at them as mere words without meaning. This couldn't be further from the truth.

They take their obligations as something irrelevant, as mere show or something that has very little meaning if any at all. They fail to realize that they have committed themselves before their Brethren and their God to be held responsible for the violation of their obligations. So they lie on bended knees in front of their Brothers and ultimately their God.

I guess no one has explained to them that Freemasonry is a moral institution based on the highest standards known to mankind. That we are bound by the moral and divine law of our faith, and that we are not only bound by our obligations but that we are also Charged to be good citizens and to conform to the laws of the country in which we live.

One of the best demonstrations of the commitment necessary from the individual to the Fraternity is best expressed in the Ancient Charges where it admonishes the Master Mason that "You are bound by duty, honour and gratitude to be faithful to your trust, to support the dignity of your character upon every occasion and to enforce by precept and example, obedience to the tenets of Freemasonry."

This would make you wonder what the repercussion would be for his violations—well probably none. If this surprises you, look around and see how many things get swept under the rug. How many Brothers are willing to take the violator's side, offer tons of excuses for their bad behavior thinking that any punishment would be an injustice? This could be simply because they are also of the same belief that these were just mere words, hollow promises, and too old to mean anything.

Then we have Brothers who under no circumstance would be caught dead violating any part of their obligations, who have been pillars of rectitude and morally pure. They wonder where our Fraternity is going but fail to denounce this type of behavior because they are waiting for someone else to do it for them.

To these Brothers as much as I love and respect them, I would also like to remind them of something I have said for many years. It is indicative of our society today where very little personal involvement is demonstrated when good people see bad things happening and turn a blind eye for fear of getting personally involved in anything they may consider controversial or something that would put them out and that is; "Evil succeeds where good is indifferent."

My Brothers, this is why they can get on their knees and

lie, because by our lack of action we have said welcome to the deceivers, frauds & cheats that knock on our doors to have them desecrate our Altar, populate our Fraternity, and violate everything we hold dear.

Remember these individuals were charged to practice those great moral lessons that were taught in the Lodge. However the practice is different, and it reflects on all of us because their conduct while wearing a ring, a shirt or in their social media loudly says that they are members of the Fraternity of Masons while their conduct leaves a lot to be desired thereby discrediting this great and noble Institution.

Today more than ever we can by our upright conduct and moral rectitude attract men in our society that are looking for just that type of atmosphere or we can allow the deceivers, frauds and cheats to continue to attract the lowest common denominator among our society by the way they advertise their membership in our Fraternity.

Masonry is a way of life, and must be practiced in our society by those of us who breathe it, feel it, and live it. It is what we do in our daily lives among our fellow citizens that makes the difference and demonstrates that we are Masons by the way we deal with them squarely, honestly, and compassionately. If you want to make Freemasonry relevant you need to practice it in your daily lives. Remember that failure to do just that may reflect dishonor to the Fraternity.

We are all charged to be our Brothers keepers and we need to whisper wise counsel in our Brothers ears when any deviation in behavior is perceived. At the same time we need to report to our Vigilance Committee and up the Fraternal structure any violation of civil law and un-masonic behavior. You must not consider you are finished in your involvement after reporting, but stay engaged and follow up to make sure those in charge fulfill their obligations.

This may come to you as a shock, it is NOT! However, all of those in the leadership position in our Fraternity, regardless of what level, may not be too eager to do the right thing for Freemasonry and follow up on the violators.

As for those in the Lodges, it has been my experience that very few Lodges can conduct an investigation or trial in a fair and equitable manner. In most cases you have a polarization of the Lodge in one way or the other depending on the individual.

Some will convict and punish severely if the Brother is someone that has made himself a nuisance regardless of the infraction, while others will exonerate anyone that has ingratiated himself regardless of how severe the infraction.

The same happens for the Grand Lodges which look at the cost of the cases as a scary thing that places a drain on their finances. With more and more Brothers willing to challenge their authority it has caused a real alarm and shyness in some Grand Bodies from following through on the principles that Freemasonry itself stands for, which should never be negotiated.

I was astonished when many have argued that we could not afford to stand on our principles because of the cost of litigation, and that the insurance companies would want to negotiate a settlement, falling into the pitfall of selling out on our principles which must never be compromised under any circumstance.

Compounded with the leadership's inability to recognize that the more they shy away from enforcing the law the more the lawbreakers are emboldened. Those that will stand steadfast by our principles diminish in number because they see the conduct of their leaders and it outrages them with their failure to act against the offenders.

You would think that the Grand Lodges have a better grasp than those of the Lodges. In reality they are a reflection of the Lodges in behavior and conduct, with very little stomach to deal with a growing problem, which in my estimation is caused by the Deceivers, Frauds & Cheats we allowed into our Lodges while they lie at our Altars.

For too long our Fraternal side has been ignored at all levels. If this Fraternity is to continue as it has been known for the last three centuries it must start getting back to basics with a strong leadership at the Grand Lodge and every other leadership position in the Craft with absolutely no tolerance for those who violate our obligations.

Outside of the symbolic penalties from times of yore, our obligations are not ambiguous and lay out the behavior expected of all Masons. This is also expanded in the Charges and the Lectures.

Why is our Fraternity haunted by these dark passages created by so many of the Deceivers, Frauds and Cheats that have entered our Fraternity? There are many reasons and they have been exposed in the previous chapters.

Further, we must hold our leadership responsible to fulfill their obligations and charge of their Office lest they also become part of the Deceivers, Frauds and Cheats who take their oath and obligations on their knees and ignore or violate them with impunity.

The question is: What do we do to correct these difficulties? The answer is very simple: "We must step up and live up to our Obligations, Charges, Lectures, Lessons, Laws, Rules and Regulations and hold everyone accountable for their actions—those who violate them as well as those who turn a blind eye to them.

We need to expect nothing but full enforcement of the Laws by our own leaders at the Lodge and Grand Lodge level lest they suffer the scorn of the Craft for their failure and possibly face a tribunal of their peers. That is, if there would be someone with enough courage, fortitude, and rectitude of conduct to carry out his obligations and Oath of Office.

They lied on their knees and most turn a blind eye to it. May the Great Architect of the Universe help us all!

Chapter 7

Where Do We Go From Here?

"Freemasonry is an establishment founded on the benevolent intention of extending and conferring mutual happiness upon the best and truest principles of moral life and social virtue."
—Â Â CALCOTT

Now that we have a Brother well on his way to becoming a just and upright man and Mason we must now make use of his time. Time is the most precious commodity each of us possesses. It is so precious that no amount of money or wealth can buy back the time that has passed. Therefore we must be careful not to misuse our time and more especially someone else's time.

As a matter of course we know that our Masonic Lodges will confer Degrees and bring members into our Lodges. Therefore we must always be ready to bring these Brothers into the fold.

During the course of the Degrees and hopefully their attendance to the Lodge, as expressed in the previous chapter, we now have built a bond with these Brothers. If we haven't, unfortunately we are behind the curve and must move fast before we lose them if we haven't already done so. The importance of building ties cannot be stressed enough. This will bind these Brothers to us in a way that nothing else will and if we fail, these Brothers will continue to look for what they came here in search of somewhere else, if we cannot meet their needs.

Time is of the essence and we have a limited amount of it in which we can accomplish our task and make good on our promise of "making good men better." Therefore we must have a plan upon the Trestle Board on how we will be dealing with these Brothers so they too can find the great Principles and Tenets of our Fraternity and allow them to guide all their future undertakings by these principles among men and Masons alike.

The designs on this Trestle Board must address the needs of the Candidates who were drawn by the slogan of "making good men better."

Although we have used this slogan for many years and for me I have heard of it since I became a Master Mason over 30 years ago, there is no real road map that plots this life long journey. While I understand that this journey is personal, we should give these Brothers a starting point, a set of guidelines, and assistance in this journey to a better way of life.

The starting point was when we provided a Mentor to guide this future Brother through his entire initiation Entered Apprentice to Master Mason. Secondly, we follow the guidelines as outlined in a later chapter for mentoring and thirdly we have laid out a study guide for his quest for knowledge.

The first two would have been laid out during the mentoring process. It is the third step we have to continue to work on, not just with the recently Raised Brothers but with the entire membership of the Lodge. This will ensure that the Brothers continue to seek more enlightenment. The more light the closer to perfection, the closer to perfection, the closer to the Great Architect of the Universe, the closer we get to "making a good man better."

This can be easily attained and something our Symbolic Lodges have given up for whatever reason. They have allowed the Appendant Orders to take over what was historically and rightfully originated in the Symbolic Lodge.

It was the Symbolic Lodges that created the environment where men of great ideas were willing to discuss their thoughts and pose their arguments either pro or con to the different philosophies of the time. It was here that great minds of the Enlightenment Era furthered the ambiance of continued learning where ordinary men could not find it otherwise.

Although we have many competing entities in Masonry I can assure you that the highest Degree that can be attained is the Master Mason's Degree. Nothing is higher than this, because regardless of whatever order you may belong to, they all predicate their membership on their members being Master Masons. None of them stand alone. They built their edifice on our foundation. No foundation, No edifice.

Although they are rich in title and numerical orders one has to look into the background of their origination and proliferation of its degrees in Europe as well as in the Americas, more especially in the United States, where they did not encounter any political or religious persecution as in Latin America.

Just think of all the centuries prior to 1717 when Operative Masons existed, gathered in Lodges, conducted the work and improved men's lives by teaching them a trade, which made them the first self-improvement society in the world where common men were allowed privileges only reserved for those who were involved in both celestial and terrestrial powers.

Look at that period of time since 1717 and you will find that many of these Appendant Orders did not begin until many years after. Regardless of their numbering, titles and degrees they came much later, building on what Masonry had achieved.

No doubt, they try to continue in the same manner taken from Freemasonry. Some may like their numerical system or hierarchy but none come close to the Symbolic Lodge's system which at times may be contradicting their own structure.

These Appendant Bodies continue to make statements that they have a higher learning of a philosophical superiority although many admit that there is nothing higher than the Three Degrees of Freemasonry. They continue to sell it as if they would complete what was started in the Symbolic Lodges.

However, if properly thought through, you may see that the Symbolic Lodge starts a candidate and it may take him anywhere between three to nine months, with six being the average, to have the Three Degrees conferred on a Candidate. If properly conveyed with mentoring, education, and catechisms it would probably take the longest of time.

All the while it is conveying to the Candidate the message that Masonry is a never-ending study of life itself. It is the application of the moral lessons taught in Masonry to one's individual life that we can become better men, allowing us to continue to build on our own Temple whose completion will be when we lay down our working tools on that lonely walk towards that undiscovered country, that house not made with hands eternal in the heavens, where the Grand Architect of the Universe will welcome us with these words "well done good and faithful fellow."

Yet, these institutions of so called higher learning intent to convey on a one single day class or two day class all the philosophical knowledge that can be imparted on one individual by exemplifying a hand full of degrees out of the many with an exemplar representing a large class, thereby having none of the experience of firsthand knowledge.

There is nothing that these Appendant Orders give that one cannot receive in the Symbolic Lodge with the exception of the titles, words, grips and numbering system of their internal structure. The philosophy of the order is for each and every one to seek for themselves as an independent free thinker, to conduct their own studies to build on what they had begun, to expand their horizon to take that journey towards that ever bright and everlasting light of knowledge.

The growth has to be individual and personal. No one can do it for you, for if that is done you will stop being the independent free thinker that came into Masonry seeking to make himself better, not a clone of one particular individual regardless of how bright he might have been or is. Masonry intends to make good men better by their own personal quest, dedication and commitment to take that journey of their own free will and accord, not to take another person's word for it.

Today more than ever one can do all the necessary research with the amount of work available on paper and the internet and compare all of the different and competing philosophies without depending on any one single individual, but have them all at his fingertips. Study the mysteries of the Mystic Art, and the founding documents of this beautiful Fraternity against the claims of the others and compare the need and the differences between the Symbolic Lodges and the Appendant Orders not only as it relates to the States but to the world. You will be amazed by what you find and the importance of preserving Freemasonry, true and unimpaired.

The Symbolic Lodge system as it stands is complete and needs no further expansion or explanation, no further degrees. It existed before 1717 with no competition. In its nearly half to first century of contemporary existence it stood alone fully and complete. It was those that for lack of understanding, self-aggrandizement, love of titles and recognition contrary to what Freemasonry teaches, who built other distractions in order for them to have a place within the institutions social status or simply the opportunity to enrich themselves.

In the Symbolic Lodge the completion of the spiritual Temple is an allegory for the individual Mason working on himself and only through self-improvement could that temple be completed. Which work has to be of his own free will and accord; free thinkers that will improve themselves in Masonry converting the rough ashlar into the perfect ashlar?

We don't want to cast any aspersions on any of the Allied and Appendant Orders, we just simply want to state some facts as they relate to the Symbolic Lodges and its rightful place, supreme and not subordinate to any other entity that may or may not consider itself Masonic or Masonic affiliated or dependent. I'm personally a perpetual member of the Rites and have participated in their degrees, held offices and received honors, all of which I'm very proud of.

Symbolic Masonry is the one and only true University of Freemasonry where its Masonic philosophy is taught to its members, through Symbols, Rituals and Lectures, and the inherent inquisitiveness of the Mason in search of Further Light. This University has no graduates, as it is a lifelong career of learning and dealing with life's trials and tribulations and the application of the Masonic Principles and Tenets taught in its hallowed halls inculcating in us of our duties to guide our actions by the Masonic way of life.

The question that we started with at the opening of this chapter still remains. Where do we go from here? The answer is simple—back to basics.

We make the Symbolic Lodge what it was always intended to be—an environment for learning and discussion of the principles and tenets that separate us form all other organizations whether Appendant or not.

We are engaged in our order by practicing our principles and tenets. We fulfill our civic duties as inculcated in our rituals and obligations as free men and thinkers as the Great Architect of the Universe gives us the light to see it for ourselves, not told by someone or some entity.

We change our approach to membership concentrating on quality not quantity. This is the only way that we will start drawing a larger number of good men that appreciate the principles of our institution. As long as we keep lowering our standards we will continue to widen the gap between the good men and us. We need to keep our Fraternity unsoiled and unimpaired.

We need to create that Masonic Experience that can be absorbed by all the senses, with a great number of sideliners, great dinners, great Rituals, and great fellowship. This should be followed by a continued involvement in the Lodge all the way through the Three Degrees with mentoring, education and catechism. This is what makes Masons and builds the bonds that bind us as one Brotherhood of men under the Fatherhood of God.

We must simply get back to basics and stick by the

orthodoxy that was set out when the Grand Lodge movement was created. Promote what the Institution was intended to be through education and practice it like it was intended to be practiced, without adding to it or taking away from it.

We must be committed to truly practicing its core values of universality and belief in a Supreme Being, dedicating ourselves to making good men better through education, discussion and exchange to practice the core tenets and principles without innovation.

This approach if properly implemented based on our principles cannot err, and we will see a turn around and a new dawn as we approach our third centennial. Will it be easy? Probably not, but nothing worth doing is ever easy. Will it be rewarding? You bet, because anytime we make a change of the magnitude we need to make it is always rewarding. And last but not least, we will secure our posterity's future and fulfill our obligations assuring our Fraternity one more generation.

Frankly, the lack of intestinal fortitude demonstrated by some of the leadership, which does nothing and maintains the status quo, or simply doesn't understand the core values of this Fraternity and tries to change because they equate quantity with quality, has gone too far. This has led our Fraternity down the wrong path for the last several decades by lessening the requirements and converting the experience of a Masonic Journey for knowledge into a thoughtless Drive-Thru of ignorance.

This trend must be turned around. Since the leadership is failing in their responsibilities the Craft must take up the slack and demand changes by informing the leadership of the changes needed, or rising up to the occasion and becoming the leader we so desperately need.

Chapter 8

Setting Them To Work With Proper Instruction For Their Labor

"Perhaps the most valuable result of all education is the ability to make yourself do the thing you have to do, when it ought to be done, whether you like it or not. This is the first lesson to be learned."
—*Thomas Henry Huxley.*

The Lodge Communication should be one where once the essential business of the Lodge is taken care of, old and new business is discussed. The rest of the time must be dedicated to learning, fellowship, and spiritual growth.

There is nothing more important to the thinking man than time. If his time is put to good use and if he is learning, enjoying the fellowship, and experiencing spiritual growth while attending Lodge, you will insure his attendance to the Lodge as you have created something that he will be looking forward to being a part of.

There is no doubt that a great part of our culture is interested in getting from "point a" to "point b" faster than

Google can conduct a search. However, Freemasonry is a tortoise in a hare's world and for good reasons. Masonry is dedicated to be a lifelong study of one individual competing against self for greater improvement, one deficiency at a time, while working towards improving the inward and outward man physically, intellectually, and spiritually.

The culture created thus far in most Lodges has evolved into reading the minutes, petitions, charity, something called Masonic Education (if any, which in most cases is an oxymoron), close and go home. We have totally gotten away from what we had that made our Lodges the envy of all institutions and attracted so many illustrious men whom we still cherish and boast about. However, the reality is that since the period of enlightenment we have been on a slippery slope and every decade or generation we attract less and less illustrious individuals, with few exceptions, simply because we have failed to adhere to our founding tenets and principles.

We slice away at those tenets and principles in order to attract more individuals who are less qualified. This in turn continues to keep those individuals we would like to attract at a greater distance since they can see at a glance that we are abandoning what could have possibly attracted them into our Fraternity.

To me in our world today we have lost or fail to understand the definition of the very word "Fraternity" that we are a part of, which is defined as: "Fraternity (Latin frater: "brother") is a brotherhood, although the term sometimes connotes a distinct or formal organization and sometimes a secret society. A fraternity (or fraternal organization) is an organized society of men associated together in an environment of companionship and brotherhood; dedicated to the intellectual, physical, and social development of its members." (http://en.wikipedia.org/wiki/Fraternity)

As you can see by the definition above together with previous statements, it is easy to see that while we continue our downward spiral, all is not that bad. If while we are doing so, we start to correct that which took us down and prepare a culture whereby they are eliminated and corrective measures are introduced to turn the situation around.

We do this by being more selective in the material that we recommend, by looking well into the recommenders and questioning the reasons why their candidate will be a good addition to the Craft. Respecting the universality of our Craft must be a paramount observance. What would this individual bring to the Craft that would qualify him as a candidate for further light and also raise the make-up quality of our Fraternity?

Next we must provide the vehicle for a journey where the individual would improve himself by providing an atmosphere of friendship and Brotherly Love, dedicated to the intellectual, physical, spiritual, and social advancement of our members within our Lodges.

Only the Lodges that allow time for these events to take place foster the opportunity to create Masons. Otherwise you are making members, who unfortunately are wasting their time and money for the opportunity to belong to a good ole boys club and carry a dues card to something they cannot articulate or even begin to understand, using that old cliché: "if I tell you, I have to kill you" to hide their unfortunate self-induced ignorance.

Before we set them to work we must work on the physical building itself so it can deliver the atmosphere required for proper learning as well as deliver a message to the Craft itself, of creating an orderly world for themselves, for their individual building efforts outside of the Lodge, whereby body and mind are harmonized as one.

So let us create an atmosphere where clutter, dirt, noise and darkness are eliminated. A place where we can be comfortable within ourselves providing a conversational setting where everyone can hear and exchange ideas without fear of embarrassment, or of feeling left out.

Whether we have a library in the Lodge or not let us ask the Brothers to share their books with us if they are not using them anymore and not let them sit unused in some box or shelf gathering dust. Let us create a system in our Lodges where Brothers can borrow books and return them for other Brothers to use, but also let's ask them to rate the book and ask if they would recommend such a book to another Brother for their reading. This would be a great benefit if it can be done within the Lodge communication, not only to demonstrate the use of the library, but also to continue to encourage the Brothers to read. Also it may be good to announce the name of Brothers that are using the library and keep as part of the records for two purposes—to encourage the Brother that is reading as well as to let others know that this is available and keep track of who is borrowing the books.

One of the things we hope is for our Brothers to improve within themselves the ability to carry on a conversation in public without being afraid, embarrassed or feeling out of place in front of a gathering. This will give them that opportunity and allow them to grow.

Next we need to provide and encourage an ambiance where these discussions can take place within the context of the Lodge to improve our combined intellect mentally and spiritually from the discussions presented, and inspire others to do the same.

The members of the Lodge should provide and recommend a list of material for reading for their personal use which may serve as a guideline for their Masonic edification and growth.

The Lodge must be an oasis of peace and tranquility which fosters everything that is good in Masonry where good fellowship and Brotherly Love are not just something that is talked about but something felt by all involved.

The designs upon the Trestle Board should be those that contain all the elements necessary to further the study of Masonry in your Particular Lodge.

Part of the study should include a period of fellowship that facilitates further individual discussions of the subject or other matter in a more relaxed atmosphere. If breaking bread is included the better it will be, so the Brothers can unwind and share their experiences in a friendlier setting.

Preferably this should happen at the end of the study session or meeting, always remembering the ancient Masonic charges which state:

THE CHARGES

OF

A FREEMASON

Extracted from

The Ancient Records of Lodges Beyond the Sea, and of Those in England, Scotland and Ireland, For the Use of the Lodges in London

To be Read at the Making of New Brethren, or when the Master shall order it.

VI. OF BEHAVIOR, VIZ.:

5. Behavior at Home, and in your Neighborhood

"You are to act as becomes a moral and wise man; particularly, not to let your family, friends, and neighbours know the concerns of the Lodge, etc., but wisely to consult your own honour, and that of the ancient Brotherhood, for reasons not to be mentioned here. You must also consult your health, by not continuing together too late, or too long from home, after Lodge hours are past; and by avoiding gluttony or drunkenness that your families be not neglected or injured, nor you disabled from working."

We must never make the Lodge an excuse for our shortcomings or any excess in our conduct which may discredit our Lodge and our Fraternity and more especially with our loved ones or anyone that would count on our behavior being that of an upright and honorable man.

On the business side a competent Lodge is one that follows strict obedience to the rules and regulations of your particular jurisdiction fully and completely without reservations of any kind, thereby serving as an example to its own members to obey the rules and regulations of the Lodge and Jurisdiction.

The Master and Officers of the Lodge should encourage the membership at large to participate in all aspects of the Lodge and in their particular committees giving the Brothers attending the Lodge an opportunity to serve the Craft. When appointing a Brother to a committee the Officer should consult the Brother prior to the appointment, as not to place him in an embarrassing situation.

With our Lodges bringing in new material every year and the rush to place those newly raised Brothers in some sort of progressive line which lacks stability in many cases. We need to constantly remind our Brothers of the duties of the Officers and members at large, that the Lodge may be operated according to their By-Laws.

However, most importantly we need to set proper designs upon our Trestle Board for the Craft to succeed. The rush must be slowed down or stopped, the decline in knowledge must be curbed otherwise we will fail in our mission to leave our posterity a functional Fraternity.

This can be accomplished by following the guidelines of your jurisdiction. If your jurisdiction does not have a set of guidelines this may be a great project to start and then present to your Grand Lodge for approval and acceptance or simply adopt them for your Lodge guidelines. It is not that hard to do. There is so much information available to pick from and adopt whatever you may need in order to make your set of guidelines. Just make sure it meets within the confines of your particular jurisdiction's laws, rules and regulations.

As a practicing Mason you should have in your possession the following books for you particular jurisdiction and this is a fine way to start your personal library. These are the Book of Constitutions of your Particular Grand Lodge, Your Lodges By-Laws and a set of your Jurisdiction History Books if available to enhance all of the booklets you have had given to you on your way to becoming a Master Mason.

While trying to master the business side of the Lodge, which is important, you must continue to work on your Masonic Light. I would hope that by now you would have a list of reading material that your particular jurisdiction may recommend. If not there are sources to look when trying to find a list and since the subjects vary greatly from esoteric to jurisprudence, from symbolism to particular rites, from historical to poetry, I'm sure you will find your niche.

One thing I would suggest is to read about our humble beginnings and understand the purpose of Masonry. Although many look at it as a good ole boys club, I assure you, such is not the case. We have purpose and meaning, understanding them will make the difference between a member and a Mason. It is up to you to choose one, I pray you choose the latter as we already have too many of the first.

Once you have read and understand our meaning and our purpose I pray you will become like our Operative Brothers who dedicated their life to building edifices and spreading knowledge of the trade. The only difference is you will be building minds and spreading the knowledge of life to build a better man, one Brother at a time.

This is a beautiful and fulfilling undertaking and the reason why we became Masons to make good men better, starting with ourselves. Have you made progress? Are you better today than when you came? If the answer is no, start today and seek help from more experienced Brothers. Do not put it off 'till tomorrow. Those things that are important need to be started in the present, not in the tomorrows. If the answer is yes, I congratulate you and I hope that man in the mirror is smiling back at you. Now help others in getting started to achieve the dream of becoming a better man.

Chapter 9

Stated Communications E.A. vs. M.M.?

Here we must start with a little historical background. Prior to 1843 the Grand Lodges in the United States conducted their business in the Entered Apprentice Degree, as did the rest of the world.

After 1826, there was a massive departure that took place that caused some Grand Lodges to go under and others to verily hold on with almost all their Lodges gone under. This anti-masonic phobia led to the Anti-Masonic Party in order to elect non-masons into offices across the U.S. This anti-masonic paranoia can only be compared to that conducted by despots trying to destroy the Craft in foreign countries.

Masonry had lost its popularity. There were very few Masons that stuck with it and much less, spoke on its behalf. The following decade became a rough and rugged road to travel, and by the 1840's Masons were on the move to make changes to prevent this from ever happening again and strengthening our Institution.

It was in 1843 that the Baltimore Convention was held on

an appeal of the Grand Lodge of Alabama to its sister Grand Lodges in 1839, which paved the road to this all-important event that would help shape Masonry and the Grand Lodges of the United States 'till present day.

On May 8, 1843, fifteen (some have reported sixteen) of the twenty-three American Grand Lodges attended this convention in Baltimore, Maryland, a greater representation of almost 65 per cent, from less than the 50 per cent that had gathered in 1842 for the same purpose. The Grand Lodges agreed on the work presented the previous year and adopted the items below as recommendations to the Grand Lodges which profoundly changed Masonry forever in the United States.

1. They adopted the Webb Monitor with minor changes in the Ceremony of Installation and the due guards for the Second and Third Degrees according to Brother Jensen: "… changed and made to conform to that of the first degree in position and explanation."

2. Also, the convention changed the immovable jewels of the Lodge, which in the English system consisted of the Rough and Perfect Ashlars and the Trestle Board…to that of the Square, Level and Plumb Rule.

3. Introduced dues card and letter of good standing for universal use.

4. Agreed to have Subordinate Lodges to set cash fees for the Degrees and not to accept any more promissory notes.

5. Many Grand Lodges changed from conferring all business in the Entered Apprentice Degree to the Master Mason Degree.

As you have read above these subjects are sufficient in and of themselves for additional chapters but we are interested in numbers 4 & 5.

The reason for the interest in number 4 is because I'm a strong advocate that Masonry is not for everyone and that one comes to Masonry to give instead of to receive. The things we obtain from Masonry are the gratification of self-improvement, building a better man, and helping in making a better world for all. If a candidate cannot afford to pay the fees, then he is not a good candidate for Masonry as he will unfortunately be taking away from himself and his family. The duty to provide for them must come before the Fraternity.

This very practice in the States, which I have never heard or read of being practiced in any other jurisdiction outside of the U.S., could have been what lead us to the difficult events transpiring in the 1820's which spread like wildfire across the land. The membership abandoned the Craft by overwhelming numbers. It may have not been just because of the bad publicity. It may have also been because they may have not had much invested in the Fraternity—but enough of this subject. Let me focus on number 5.

The dramatic change from conducting all Lodge business in the Entered Apprentice Degree to the Master Mason Degree was indeed a change that would profoundly change Masonry in the US.

This was not achieved immediately although some Grand Lodges started implementing it in 1842 based on the previous convention discussions and others didn't even adopt until after 1851. However there is no doubt that all the Grand Lodges, new and old, were on board sometime before the turn of the century.

Although this may have given these Brothers a sigh of relief and peace of mind to limit the exposure, possibly preventing another crisis, it changed the Craft. Perhaps the change was not necessarily for the better as it alienated the very same people we were trying to attract.

Just think of yourself joining an organization and being told in front of all those present that you are now a member of such organization and to ever walk and act as such before God and Man, with one caveat— you will not be able to participate or attend this organization until you go through additional tests and trials.

Before you know it, you have developed a bond with one or maybe two people if you are fortunate, and you and they have nothing in common. You have very little contact if any with any other member of the organization until six to nine months have passed. The question to ask here is why? Why do we speak so much of fellowship and demonstrate so little of it to our new members.

If we are interested in membership—let me rephrase that—if we are interested in quality membership and building better Masons we need to start conducting our business in the Entered Apprentice Degree, where all of our members are welcome. We say that once you are an Entered Apprentice Mason you are always a Mason. Then why do we treat them like anything but a Mason by keeping them away from a business meeting that has nothing in it that an Entered Apprentice couldn't participate in?

I know we place a lot of emphasis on the Master Mason Degree because of the events that transpired at the Baltimore Convention. However, the rest of the world does not have the same issues and they have survived 300 years of continuous Masonic Practices.

The Mother Grand Lodge of the World, the United Grand Lodge of England, conducts their business in the following ways. This is given as an example of what can be achieved as an alternate way of conducting business as demonstrated by nearly 300 years of practice.

• The Grand Lodge, Provincial and District Grand Lodges conduct their business in Ancient form in the Master Masons Degree.

• English Lodges are always opened in the Entered Apprentice Degree. The business of the Lodge is conducted only in the First or E.A. Degree. If the Lodge is passing a Brother to the Second Degree, the Lodge is then opened in the Second or Fellow Craft Degree. If a Brother is being raised to the Sublime Degree of a Master Mason, it must first be opened in the E.A. Degree, then opened in the F.C. Degree and then in the Third or Master Mason Degree. The same is true when stepping down the Lodge. It closes the M.M. Degree and reopens in the F.C. Degree, then closes the F.C. Degree and reopens in the E.A. Degree. (Ritual requirements for stepping up and down are simpler.)

• With respect to the Entered Apprentices, they have a vote and can hold office. They also have a say and are considered full members of the Lodge and UGLE. They are presented with the Book of Constitutions, the By-Laws of the Lodge, a copy of the Volume of the Scared Law and the Ritual of the First Degree at their initiation.

• An Entered Apprentice can vote on all matters regularly brought before the Lodge. He can also propose candidates and vote on any Brother applying to join his Lodge. He can also be appointed to Office in the Lodge at the decision of the W.M. who appoints all his Officers, except the Treasurer, who together with the W.M., are the only two elected Officers in the Lodge.

• A Grand Lodge Certificate will not be issued until the E.A has Passed to the Fellow Craft Degree and Raised to the

Sublime Degree of a Master Mason, or as they prefer to call it, the Second and Third Degree.

This would be a great way to conduct the business of our Lodges and still maintain the fellowship of all those men we bring as Entered Apprentice and Fellow Craft into our midst and let true Fellowship and Brotherly Love prevail amongst the Craft.

There are currently sixteen Grand Lodges in the U.S., the last time I checked, that have provisions allowing the practice of opening the Lodge in the Entered Apprentice Degree, which is left up to the Worshipful Master to decide how he runs his Lodge.

There is also a mixed bag of what the Entered Apprentice and Fellow Crafts rights are in the Lodge as far as to voice, vote and hold office in their Particular Lodges. However, the main object here is that they can attend Lodge and participate in the Lodge Fellowship.

The rest of the rights for the Entered Apprentice may come in time. Then we can safely and without bias remove our traditional hat and replace it with the hat of knowledge which deliberates with thoughts based on facts and do the right thing for our Fraternity.

At times I think we tend to change in haste and without much thought, treating the symptoms and not the cause. Without looking at the root cause of the problem we are only fooling ourselves that we are actually doing something to cure it.

The ability to practice Masonry in the Entered Apprentice Degree I believe will go a long way in cutting down the number of Entered Apprentice and Fellow Craft Masons that never return to the Lodge because they may feel disenfranchised.

There will not be a race to get to the Master Mason's

Degree since they can participate in the Lodge allowing the Particular Lodge to do a better job with Masonic Education and raising the bar of Masonic Knowledge, which seems to lack in general at all Degrees.

Not everything that is tradition is good and the conducting of the Stated Meetings in the Master Mason Degree is only one of them. It is up to you to reason with the facts and become the change you want to see in your particular jurisdiction and preserve Masonry the way it was intended to be from time immemorial.

Chapter 10

Ritual!

"Good ritualistic work is a beauty to behold.
But it can only be good if it is rehearsed many times."
—Unknown

Masonry has many variations of the ritual. As a matter of fact not all Grand Lodges have an adopted ritual allowing their Particular Lodges to use various Rituals that have been practiced for close to a couple of centuries in their jurisdiction.

Nonetheless, whether the ritual is the same for the whole jurisdiction or not is not important. The types of Ritual or Rituals used do not make a difference; the difference is made on how the ritual is delivered.

One of the differences between us and other fraternal organizations is the Ritual. Our Ritual is so important and has impressed so many men that many other organizations have copied or tried to imitate portions of our Ritual.

Whether we have adopted work or not, and whether we are in our own jurisdiction or not, when we see any Masonic Ritual we can certainly understand it with whatever differences we may find and know what is going on and feel comfortable with the Degree being conferred. As a personal observation we will be in full understanding of the Degree being conferred regardless of the Ritual or language being used to deliver the Degree.

Our Ritual has been always intended to be delivered with dignity and with the best ritualist available for this most important Masonic milestone in the Candidate's Masonic life. The solemnity of this ceremony cannot be overstated as the Three Degrees of Freemasonry are intended to deliver lifelong lessons in Morality, Conduct, Integrity, and Dignity, and a sense of admiration to our Creator, none of which should ever be taken lightly if you are truly going to make yourself a better man.

Our Fraternity has always been an Initiatic Institution that places a great deal of importance on this aspect of our order. To deliver the very best Degree possible must be our constant aim. If we are going to be the best we must deliver the best. We cannot talk the talk if we are not going to walk the walk. To do anything different will be hypocritical.

We must excel at conferring the Degrees; we must be ready to deliver the best performance each and every time. Then and only then will we deliver a true Masonic Experience and send the right message to the Candidate in search of light that we are the best and expect nothing less, including of him.

A Degree where the elements are used to the advantage of the Degree team—things like light, darkness, smells and silence—can be tools that will intensify the senses of the

Candidates and make his mind more receptive to what he is experiencing while the Degree is being conferred.

This will mean that the lights in the Lodge may have to be adjusted to deliver the right atmosphere to the particular part of the Degree, such as whether to use light or darkness to enhance the action being taken at any particular moment. Also the mentioning of the tapers around the altar, not light bulbs, will be more true to the ceremonies as fire has a greater meaning than 25 watt bulbs burning either fake flames, flashlights, candles, or Square and Compass bulbs which only serve to take away from the work itself and look like it doesn't matter to us whether or not we live by the ritual and its meaning.

Smells have been used in many ceremonies throughout the centuries from religious ceremonies to relaxation techniques to release stress. Here we can use incense to awaken the sense of smell. Remember the pot of incense in our Lectures, which speaks of a pure heart? Well, incense lays claim to purify the human soul and as such will help in waking up the sense of smell and set another tone to the ceremonies never experienced by the Candidate. Incense, although not a practice in the States, is used in many Grand Lodges around the world. This can be used for added value as the Candidate is entering into a different ambience for the first time in Masonry.

Last but not least is silence. Silence is that element that is awakened by the absence of noise. It intensifies your hearing and makes the individual increase his other senses to perceive any noise that may lead them to know or understand what the noise may represent and be a bit apprehensive as to what will be coming before them.

Although this will cost nothing it may be the hardest to

attain as you depend on everyone's participation in order to succeed in creating this atmosphere. Not everyone may understand the value that Silence brings to the ceremonies, especially if they did not experience the same when they received the Degrees.

In some Lodges the Degrees are delivered with much mirth and frivolity taking away from the solemn lessons they are trying to convey of morality, charity, tolerance, righteousness, personal growth, and of the different stages of manhood, which include a very important educational phase.

We must categorically deny any place and give any quarters to anyone regardless of rank that persist in this type of behavior that is undermining the lessons taught by our rituals.

Needless to say, when practicing Ritual, Usages and Customs, we must perform them according to the Laws, Rules and Regulations of your Jurisdiction.

Masons have a tendency to introduce bits and pieces of Ritual from other Jurisdictions into theirs. In many cases this is frowned upon by those Jurisdictions that have adopted specific Ritual Work and it is a violation of their laws and counterproductive in teaching and performing such Ritual because by doing so you demonstrate contempt for the rules. This is definitely a bad start.

I know of no Ritual that when delivered properly and solemnly has not been absolutely beautiful and full of glory delivering exactly the proper message on behalf of Freemasonry.

Much has been made of the Chamber of Reflection, mostly because it is not used in the American System of Symbolic Freemasonry and it is being looked at as a novelty or curiosity. Having been conferred the Three Degrees in a Clandestine Lodge in 1976, which used the Scottish Ritual (primarily used in Latin America) which used the Chamber of Reflection and having been a recipient as well as delivering the Candidate into the Chamber I can tell you the same lessons were delivered in a different form when I renounced my affiliation and petitioned a Regular Lodge and went through the entire initiation process again in 1983.

What stands out between both is that the initiatic process by far was taken more seriously and the other topics herein discussed were used more to their advantage than the average Lodge I have participated in since 1983.

We must excel at conferring the Degrees, whether the Candidate is a curiosity seeker, detractor, or pure at heart matters not since this will take time to tell. However, we are obligated to the Candidate and the Fraternity to deliver the best Degree possible, thereby ensuring the Candidate receives the Masonic Experience.

If we are able to achieve the best Degree we can and the Candidate is one who is pure at heart and is truly seeking the mysteries of the Mystic Art and wants to delve into the esoteric side of Masonry, we will have just sparked that search for light and knowledge necessary to make a Mason.

Chapter 11

Mentoring

"Tell me and I forget, teach me and I may remember,
involve me and I learn."
—Benjamin Franklin

Our leadership is so concerned with creating members that they do not look further on how to create Masons. In this chapter we will look beyond that and focus on how we can speed up the process of making Masons.

The quickest way we can create Masons to secure the future of this Ancient and Honorable Institution is through education. This will achieve a twofold purpose of creating Masons and "Making Good Men Better."

What is a Mentor? Perhaps it is the most rewarding occupation a Mason can have and discharge in the name of Masonry. Who can be a Mentor? Any Brother who would like to take the role of a teacher to assist a younger Mason in achieving his rightful place in our Fraternity as a fitting block of spiritual growth and knowledge in Masonry that would assist him in becoming a better son, father, brother, and citizen.

The Mentor must be a Brother of knowledge and experience, well informed in the history of the country, state or province and Freemasonry, as well as the Grand Jurisdiction and Lodge of which he is a member. Only those that possess the highest knowledge should be given the opportunity to impart knowledge, otherwise the system will fail do to loss of confidence in the Mentor and the process.

Besides knowledge, the Mentor must also be one who is proper in conduct, speech and dress. In other words this Brother should be the epitome of a gentleman and Mason, inspiring his pupils to imitate all his qualities. We must remember that we are building living stones that will support the individual and the collective spiritual building of our Fraternity.

When does mentoring begin? Mentoring begins immediately after the candidate receives the letter informing him of his acceptance with date and time of his Initiation, proper attire for the occasion, and the name of the Mentor with his information.

Here the Mentor should contact the candidate after enough time has elapsed for him to receive the letter from the Secretary of the Lodge. In this initiatory contact the Mentor should introduce himself to the candidate and repeat the information in the letter, including what proper attire is for this important event in his life and the time to receive his first Masonic lesson prior to him being initiated.

This meeting should be conducted at the Lodge and all materials covered should correspond with the history of the Craft, the Grand Jurisdiction in which he resides and customs of the Lodge along with information which will ease his mind and calm his nerves in order for him to absorb as much of the information as possible that will be presented to him.

"Warning: if your Grand Jurisdiction has a program to follow for the education and mentoring of the Candidates by all means you must follow their instructions and view these suggestions as a means to inculcate the importance of education and mentoring brought to the Candidate."

After the Candidate has received the Degree, the first order of business should be a meeting with the Mentor who will present to him a synopsis of what he has gone through and answer any questions the Candidate may have regarding the Entered Apprentice Degree.

At this time he should be presented with any information the Grand Jurisdiction may have pertaining to the Entered Apprentice Degree. He should also be informed of Lodge meetings and invited for dinners and fellowship. If the Lodge has more Entered Apprentices and Fellow Crafts they should also be invited to the Lodge. After the Master Masons have gone into the Lodge room they can either go home or remain in the Lodge and form study groups pertaining to the Degree they have been conferred and practice their catechism and expound on their reading material and experiences of the Craft thus far.

Here we must say that follow-up on any material given for reading is essential and much emphasis must be placed on the reading of such material, otherwise he will fail in improving himself if he does not expose himself to the printed word. Furthermore continued importance must be placed on the vast material available for reading as he progresses in the further Degrees in Masonry, creating in him a thirst for knowledge in anticipation of when he can have access to all the information in Symbolic Masonry.

The Mentor should be communicating with this newly Initiated Brother regarding any Degrees, as well as any other event which he can attend to start building a custom of participation and travel as well as learning the importance of fellowship with other Brothers and Lodges, including his family whenever appropriate and possible.

This process should be repeated as he advances through the Fellow Craft and Master Mason, with the appropriate information and lessons taught according to the Degree of which he is entitled to receive. Remember that the intent here is to keep this Brother engaged as well as to impart that knowledge of which he is entitled to receive, always instilling in him that soon he will reach the Sublime Degree of a Master Mason where he would be able to receive all the secrets of Masonry.

After the receiving of the Third and Last Degree of Masonry, and all the lessons of that Degree have been communicated, the focus should first be on Masonic Etiquette, afterwards which the Lodge should present this Brother with his first Masonic book to continue to encourage him to read and further his knowledge in Masonry.

At the same time the Mentor can introduce the Brother to the Lodge Library and continue to do follow up on his reading material and engage him with questions on the material with discussion to further his knowledge and his reading.

The Mentor or Mentors can further grow these Brothers into a study group to expand their knowledge and horizons to get them comfortable in exchanging information among themselves and in public speaking.

This can lead to presentations in open Lodge with possible questions and answers thus preparing these Brothers to become Mentors themselves passing the torch of leadership to those who are coming behind us and securing our legacy for future generations. This can also assist the Brother to develop and improve his public speaking skills and how to engage in civil discourse with others in a public forum.

If the program is executed as explained and within the rules and regulations of your Grand Jurisdiction it will make the difference between members and Masons. Remember that an "Educated Mason is a Dedicated Mason."

Final word for the Mentor—not that it may need to be mentioned, but since we have touched on so many topics I might as well talk about the material being discussed.

When entering into a discussion in which you are not sure, make it known to the Brother that you must first look into it and you will get back to him with the information. You must, otherwise you will lose his respect.

The same can be said for giving erroneous information lest you risk your credibility and that of the Fraternity. We do not and must not exaggerate, embellish or enhance our history, rituals, lessons benefits or traditions.

Today if you give information it would take the Candidate or Brother but a couple minutes of search on the internet to find the correct answer. Be cautions in your statements. Truth must be always present and the foremost cornerstone of our Fraternity.

Chapter 12

Masonic Education

"An Educated Mason Is A Dedicated Mason"
—Unknown

As Freemasonry's Ritual became more of the focus and gained greater importance in our Fraternity, Masonic Education took a back seat to it and it has not recovered since.

This was a gradual change in the 19th Century, and by the middle of the 20th Century many in our leadership were realizing that something had to be done and Masonic Education programs had already been popping up. In my state it started in the 1950's and I'm sure in other states with more active membership and well known Masonic scholars it might have started earlier.

Nonetheless, the importance of recognizing this symptom and the need to correct it had started with a step in the right direction being taken; if we could only follow through with it. This proved to be easier said than done.

Although we have had many Brothers in leadership roles that believed and understood this to be a serious problem, there have not been enough of them nor sufficient consistency focused on promoting Masonic Education to make a real dent in the problem. It has been more of a hit and miss approach.

Yet we have had many Brothers who have dedicated a great part of their Masonic career to educate the Craft by developing many types and volumes of Masonic information devoted to educate and expand Masonic knowledge, which is available in most Grand Lodges and the Masonic Service Association. Not to mention the great number of Masonic authors who have written thousands of volumes on Freemasonry.

This diverse information is compiled in historical narratives and accounts, symbolic explanations of the different rituals and ceremonies, alchemy, mysteries, theories, poetry, music, biographies, managerial information, how-to's for various functions of the Lodge, planning guides, and basically covering every possible and conceivable subject.

However, the average Mason barely reads any information provided him during the course of going through the Degrees and furthermore there is a very poor performance on behalf of the average Lodge to assist, promote and encourage Masonic Education. Some Brothers do not understand the difference between Masonic Education and Masonic Ritual and since proficiency is needed to advance, the focus is placed on this feature of the Fraternity.

Although some states require that Masonic Education is provided and mandated by regulations, many Lodges do not follow the guidelines, violating the rules and ignoring the importance of this valuable side of our Fraternity. The Craft in general is not demanding of the Lodge Officers to follow the rules or volunteering to perform these services for their fellow Brothers.

Another difference in the treatment of Masonic Education by those in charge is that they give this very important job to Brothers who are not qualified to perform this duty simply based on their lack of education and preparedness making a mockery out of this essential and vital part of the Craft. In many cases this places the presenter at a disadvantage where the participants are more knowledgeable than those in charge and sets the program up for failure before it even starts.

The failure to educate does not stop with the mishandling of this duty by Lodge Officers, but you can continue to go up the ladder to the Brothers in charge of the program at the District or State Level that fail to push forward the agenda and report the actual failure of the program at those levels. This is not to say that all of these Brothers fail at their job because this would not be correct. There are Brothers that work zealously to promote and nurture Masonic Education at any cost. However, their efforts go unrecognized by those that place them in charge, and give no assistance or importance to the work being achieved or the lack thereof.

Herein lies the problem. Those who are in charge are not placing sufficient importance on this program and in many cases some lip service is given but very seldom is it taken seriously. This may be because they themselves do not see the value of this educational side of our fraternity, and it may just simply be because they had never been exposed to it, and personally don't have an appreciation for it. Nonetheless the status quo seems to prevail in what is the decaying of Masonic Education.

One of my favorite Masons of the twentieth century and

Masonic luminary is M∴W∴ Dwight L. Smith, P.G.M. & P.G.S. of the Grand Lodge of Indiana. He is probably not well known outside of Indiana in today's world but is someone whom I would recommend to anyone that is in the leadership role—whether at Lodge, District or Grand Lodge—to read his writings. This Brother dedicated nearly forty years of his life to the service of the Craft in his state and other national organizations and was part of the leadership in both for nearly the same time.

In his writings he speaks on a myriad of topics giving Masonry an open, broad and unbiased analysis of the state of the Craft, looking at the then present situation, where it was heading and where it should be heading. This comes not only from his vast understanding and experience but based on actual events of which he had firsthand knowledge. These assessments where compiled during the 60's and 70's and are more true today than he could have possibly imagined, since the leadership has not addressed these matters with any consistency whatsoever.

In addressing Masonic Education he reminded the Brothers of Indiana, and this applies to Brothers the world over, of their Masonic duties stated at every opening and closing of the Lodge which is "to set the Craft to work and give them good and wholesome instruction for their labors." The Worshipful Master is the one responsible to deliver on that commitment.

He further alludes to the Past Master's Degree wherein the Worshipful Master pledges not to open or close a Lodge "without giving a lecture or section of a lecture for the edification of the Craft," concluding that the Master of the Lodge is duty bound to educate for as long as he rules and governs his Lodge.

Based on this simple obligation the Worshipful Master is responsible for the success or failure of this awesome responsibility, yet most don't realize it. The leadership above him does not assist him in most cases to accomplish this important duty: or if he fails in his duties after assistance is provided due to negligence, it is ignored by those in charge. The message delivered to the Craft by the leadership that these obligations and commitments are nothing but hollow promises from their point of view, rendering yet another serious blow to Masonic Education once again but perhaps not the final blow as long as men of integrity continue to adorn the columns of Freemasonry, even if in the minority.

This very knowledgeable Brother gives us very sound advice with two do's and don'ts, which I believe are worthy of sharing with you verbatim.

The Do's
- Keep it simple. Remember the Parables in the New Testament, The Sower, The Prodigal Son, The Mustard Seed. Nothing dry, nor academic, nor philosophical in those stories. Just plain good sense that any man can understand and remember.
- Teach through symbols. That is Freemasonry's way. And it works. Don't you ever forget it. The lesson of the Square for example. And the Trowel. And the Ashlars.

The Don'ts
- Don't call your program Masonic Educations whatever you do. Not even instruction. Sugarcoat it, if you must. Call it the Round Table. Or The Smoking Room. Or the Log. Call it almost anything, just so it isn't suggestive of a classroom.
- Don't unload the whole load each time you feed the

cow. Keep your message short and to the point. Give your instruction in small doses, and see to it that those doses are phrased in simple language.

This is a good start until the Brothers are ready to move on and get involved themselves in more heavy studies on their own and seeking other Brothers of equal or greater knowledge to share in the exchange of knowledge increasing their chances of self-improvement.

M∴W∴ Smith also makes a good point when he states: "the teacher must know more than the pupil, for one thing. But that isn't all. Instruction in Freemasonry can wreck any Lodge if it isn't planned and executed intelligently."

The assessments and recommendations of this Past Grand Master stem from the symptoms he experienced during his years of leadership positions and 40 to 50 years later I found the same symptoms during my tenure in another state, and I know it to be true in others.

Unfortunately too many Masons today follow society's simple system of no personal responsibility, getting their information from sound bites, and instant gratification, they don't read much and don't seek to do much on their own. As a matter of fact, the minute you call it education whatever it may be is dead on arrival. (Of course there are always exceptions to the rule such as the Brothers reading this book and others regardless of how small they may be.)

Regrettably most things in life that are worth attaining require personal investment with time and hard work. If it's cheaply attained and no personal sacrifices are involved they are not appreciated or are of very little value. Masonic Education needs to receive the proper worth by those who lead us and restore it to what it once was when we were in the business of making good men better.

This last statement I know will raise some eyebrows or at least I hope it does because then I have hit a cord that may make you do something if you are not doing anything in your Lodge or Grand Lodge and if you are involved I pray it may make you work harder and seek the assistance of others to turn the tide of ignorance which is so abundant within our Craft.

To my amazement I find many non-members who can sustain a Masonic discussion for or against the Fraternity and are well versed with our history, principles and humble beginnings. Of course they also know many of the conspiracy theories that are portrayed on television, from reading some of the latest fictions or from the internet. On the other hand I find Masons (not all) are better at Ritual due to the emphasis placed on it to advance to obtain the Third Degree, but have no sustainability on the others and sometimes many of the statements made are fictitious, not verifiable because the education they have received has been shoddy or delivered by teachers that didn't go the extra mile in their research or those over-zealots who embellished the facts.

For those looking for an increase in numbers of members, Masonic Education is your answer. Not lowering the standards to get new members in. You ask why? When your salesmen, which will be your current membership, cannot articulate, act or play the part of a Mason how can you recruit new members? What does that say for your organization?

All humans want to be part of a good thing, however they must perceive the value of that which they may conceive to be good. How they do this is with personal contact seeking information from a salesperson or member of whatever they seek to be a part of. If your salesperson or member cannot articulate the benefits of Masonry, its philosophies and doctrines, how can you recruit good members?

Herein lays the problem and the importance of educating our Craft that they can speak to it, but more importantly that they can live it. If we can achieve both of these goals, our problems with membership will suffer a great blow, since you will have a spokesman force to be reckoned with.

It matters not how much money you spend in radio, television or internet advertising, how many pamphlets you print or distribute, how good your websites are, if you don't have the boots on the ground that can close the deal by being able to attract instead of scare off the potential members by what they say and the way they act when they come in contact, then you are wasting your time. And even if they continue on you can find the figures that tell the story of how many drop out after the First Degree, or after a couple of years in the Fraternity. Dissatisfaction in the difference between the sales pitch and actual goods delivered is at the root of the cause.

Here again education for all concerned is the answer to our problems. We are addressing the problem but not the cause. We are focusing on the organization but not on what the organization is supposed to deliver. Understanding who we are and what we are is at the root cause of our problems. Let's get our base ready before we continue spending more funds in grandiose schemes to attract new members, or worse in changing Freemasonry in such a way that it will stop being Freemasonry in an effort to increase our membership.

Funny enough we have the system in place in most states and the MSA. Maybe in some places it may have to be tweaked. However, what we need is serious implementation. We need the same dedication and commitment to education that we have in recruitment.

Getting the base ready is fundamentally standing firm and committed to the task at hand and addressing the main causes of why our membership is not conversant in the very vocation they voluntarily chose to be a member of. Not for one year but a commitment for the long haul with the same fervor we have for recruiting numbers.

This lays at the feet of our leadership at the state level to take up this challenge and live up to their obligations and pledges. It is time for them to take their heads out of the sand and address this systemic problem that has plagued our Fraternity for more than six or seven decades.

They need to instill the importance of education and they must lead with more than just words. They need to invest time and teach by example. They can start by dedicating time on the subject of education, something the majority of Masons seem to lack in desire and dedication to really do what they profess they came here for when they reply to the following question. What came you here to do? To learn to subdue my passions and improve myself in Masonry. How ironic!

The very survival of Freemasonry depends on you and everyone else doing what we came here to do? We need YOU now more than ever if we are going to maintain Freemasonry as it was intended and not another failed social club. Stand up for our principles and the reason for our Fraternity. Once you personally understand those two simple but integral parts of who and what we are, it is time to expand your horizons whether you chose to read and discuss with others or discuss first and then read, but most importantly try to articulate until you are comfortable with establishing a conversation. This will not only fulfill your duty of improving yourself in Masonry, but it will also train you in public speaking, holding meaningful conversations, expanding your horizons, and being able to teach others by your conduct and actions.

Now you can become an ambassador or spokesperson for Masonry when it comes to speaking with the profane and answering their questions regarding membership in Freemasonry.

Now that you are conversant in Masonic matters you need to become the change you would like to see the Fraternity to be. It has been said that Masonry is a way of life. The question is— is it your way of life?

The only way to succeed in this promise is to become an enthusiastic supporter of Masonic Education. Are you? Our future depends on it.

Chapter 13

Charity

*"In Faith and Hope the world will disagree, but,
all mankind's concern is Charity."*
—*Alexander Pope*

Charity is one of those things that as I have read more,
studied it more and think about it more my position has
evolved and changed in the course of my Masonic career.

When I started in Masonry I believed that our charity
should be primarily to the Brothers and to those who came
into contact with our members and had a special need and
could be helped immediately, thus making an impact on their
life they would probably never forget.

As I progressed in my Masonic career and I became
acquainted with the other Allied and Appendant Bodies and
I saw their institutional charity my thoughts started to evolve,
thinking this was the way to go. Upon further study you
will notice two different ways of charitable giving; one that
is completely of their own and the other where they donate

to charitable corporations, which are committed to research and/or treatment of an illness that affects humanity.

More thought was given to charity in the sense that if we, the Grand Lodges of the United States, could all agree in a Charity and combine our resources we could make a greater impact as to the particular charity chosen. I worked towards this goal during my years in the Grand Line in search of a Charity that could be branded with the word Masonic in the name.

This was a goal of my fellow officers as well and we succeeded in getting other Grand Lodges involved in the concept and I thought we were onto something great for our Fraternity and on the right path.

However, the more I thought and worked with this concept, the more I saw that it was not the best way for the individual Grand Lodge to go, and started again to analyze the pros and cons as it related not to the charity but to what it would do to Freemasonry, how it would change it and the Grand Lodge participating in this endeavor.

Most Grand Lodges do not have sufficient funds to establish a charity of their own or at least to the magnitude of a hospital or research center, however they may be able to do something smaller on their own with some service to humanity.

Any one of the Grand Lodges can become a corporate sponsor of a well-known charity whether at the State or National level, however they will get lost among the many thousands of donors and may be found in the small print of a large book of donors for all their efforts receiving very little recognition if any which is the reason why they seek the partnership to begin with.

Therefore we need to be happy with our charitable work

not achieving national status in being a corporate donor as I call. It is not all is cut out to be, especially from a Masonic perspective.

During my year as Grand Master a poll was conducted of the nearly three hundred Lodges in the Jurisdiction to determine how much and who were the beneficiaries of our charity. This information was to be used during the State Legislative Session to lobby and promote our Specialty License Plate design to generate funding for the Masonic Home.

To my surprise the information that came in was wide-ranging in amounts and recipients from personal to institutional; local, state and national. And in reading the reports on where the funds were going and whom they were for or making an impact on I started to realize that my previous way of thinking was flawed in the sense that the majority of the people it impacted would not have benefited from a state or national institution. To assist individuals in need in the community in which they live who were without any other resource for assistance was the reason the Lodge had taken up this matter in the first place.

So what I found out as a result of the request was that the Lodges were really impacting an individual at the local level, fulfilling their obligations of assisting those who were less fortunate among mankind—those whom had fallen through the system and had no place to go; this is charity at its best.

The examples hit home, because what had been taught earlier in my Masonic career was coming home to roost so to speak. I remember how the local Family Services had my telephone number in order to assist them in providing quick emergency help to families in need until they could get government assistance. Let me share a few examples.

I got a call one night around 9:30 pm from Family Services asking if we could do something for a family that had three small children with twins that were less than a year old. They had not had anything to eat all day and had no food in the refrigerator or pantry. I was asked if I could do anything for them that evening or early morning until they could get the government assistance going.

or,

The call from the school teacher whose class we had adopted who asked us if we could help a child that was in desperate need of glasses but the family could not afford them, and they could not meet the requirements for government assistance, and the other children were making fun of him at school, or,

The families that were looking at Thanksgiving or Christmas with meager or no food to celebrate and with a house full of children, or,

The young person who is looking for a little help if not a complete scholarship and the local Lodge or Grand Lodge can assist with a scholarship whether large or small that will help this person achieve their dream, and the list can go on and on and on.

These are but a few samples of the importance the Lodge or Grand Lodge can provide at the local level, not to mention addressing the needs of our own members, whether at our Masonic Homes/Orphanages or at the local level, which at times are taken for granted or forgotten. More on this later.

It is for these reasons and for the teachings of our Ritual is that I must realign my thinking as to Charity from the local Lodge or Grand Lodge. We as individuals can contribute to or adopt a national charity, without having them be adopted by the Lodge or Grand Lodge as their charity.

With our small donations, and without fanfare, we can have a greater impact on any one particular person without letting the left hand know what the right hand is giving, which is the way we have been doing it for nearly 300 years and it has done us very well. As a matter of fact at the time when this Fraternity was at its highest popularity there was no corporate or organized giving by any Lodge or Grand Lodge and perhaps it should remain this way.

In analyzing corporate giving I came to the realization that we are losing our identity and ignoring the local needs. This is very real and something which very few are addressing if any, depending on the area in which you reside. This is eliminating the personal touch which is the way Masonry has made its greatest impact in society and the stories of goodwill towards mankind we hear whenever we engage in conversation with Masons and non-masons alike, or read the minutes of any Lodge, especially of days gone by.

As for our Masonic Homes/Orphanages and the individual Mason's needs, it has been said that this is our obligation, and it may very well be, but nonetheless it is an act of charity that we give to help others in need. By the way there is nothing wrong in helping or taking care of your own. Society has always looked down on those that do not take care of their own especially the male of the family. In today's colloquialism they are called "Dead Beat Dads." We should and must take care of our own and that my friend is Charity.

Also, allow me to shed a little bit of light on this subject. In my State, because we take care of our own, we free nearly two million dollars of State revenue a year that can be used to take care of more needy people—and that is Charity.

The other beautiful thing about championing Masonic Charity and not institutionalize corporate charity is that it's personal, limitless and giving with great personal satisfaction of a good deed accomplished. Let us practice Charity the Masonic way and to this I say "So Mote It Be!

Remember the old cliché that Charity begins at home and Freemasonry is the vehicle to improve individuals by making good men better and that Charity is the result of its lessons of self-improvement. Therefore keep in mind those who are less fortunate, our senior members, their widows, our orphans, a local needy Brother, a traveling Brother, a local family, or individual, a student, a child, or anyone in need that we can be of assistance.

Before we close this chapter I would like to mention the Board of Relief. The need and responsibility of the Brothers and Lodge Officers is to see that this very important committee is properly funded in order to be able to assist those in need. The Brethren at large should constantly remind the Officers of this duty, never to forget and be able to assist a worthy Brother Master Mason in distress, which is the only purpose of this committee.

Anderson's Constitutions frames this very important duty as follows:

GENERAL REGULATIONS

VII.   Every new Brother at his making is decently to clothe the Lodge, that is, all the Brethren present, and to deposit something for the relief of indigent and decayed Brethren, as the candidate shall think fit to bestow, over and above the small allowance stated by the By Laws of that Particular Lodge, which charity shall be lodged with the

Master or Wardens, or the Cashier, if the members think fit to choose one.

My Brothers, Fraternal Charity for a worthy Brother in distress is the function of the Board of Relief and the Box of Fraternal Assistance is one way to properly fund this committee and should be presented at every Stated Communication. Taking care of our own has been part of Masonry as a charity for a couple of hundred years before organized charity was introduced in America.

Chapter 14

Festive Board vs. Lodge Dinner

Festive Board a fellowship assembly in a relax atmosphere with structure and instructive conversation.
—Jorge L. Aladro

What is the difference you may ask and the answer is simply a world of difference. Many Brothers have not had the experience of Festive Board, and some call it a Table Lodge, which in many places are conducted by the Allied and Appendant Orders as a Table Chapter or Council as well.

Our Craft, from the very beginning, has been involved with meeting and dining. The meetings were something of a time of reflection, learning, respect and decorum, where the majority of the Brothers engaged in silence absorbing the information being presented by those in charge and those presenting educational information to the Craft. Remember, this was the era of the Enlighten movement, and the common man was probably being exposed to more information than man had been exposed to in the last several centuries combined.

After these meetings the Craft gather in fellowship to participate in the dining experience and there is nothing better to make great connections than that of breaking bread together. However, the Festive Board is more than just that, it is an event, a place where gentlemen gather for a ritual specially created for this purpose. It is just more than gathering in small groups around a dinner table and everyone eating at different times and doing different things, as they want. A Festive Board has structure.

The Festive Board is set up as a Lodge of antiquity where all the Brothers are facing each other and in a form that all can share what is being said and the ceremonies being conducted. There is meaning to this ritual, filled with pomp and circumstance designed to promote fellowship and enhance the dining experience. It is not an occasion for just eating; it is an occasion for celebration of fellowship and conviviality.

Although a Festive Board has structure it is not a Table Lodge where there is an opening and closing ceremony with an Altar and the Great Lights.

Most Lodges have their idiosyncrasies in style and ceremony of the Festive Board that best serves their needs with the focus being on fellowship and dining. Here the Brethren, in between the ceremonial toast and other requirements depending on their Lodge's custom, will have conversation with those around them.

This setting creates a peaceful and relaxed atmosphere where they can unwind and build relationships that will last a lifetime, strengthening the ties that bind us.

In the transformation into what some call American

Masonry we have lost many things of value to Masonry by allowing a rush in the way we do things which tends to take away all the pleasures men the world over seem to enjoy being a part of. Many blame it on the society in which we live like our needs were any different than any other industrialized nation. As a matter of fact, if we read many of our Masonic writers of the beginning of the 20th Century they were already discussing poor attendance in our Lodges, among other things.

Among the many things that have declined or been eliminated in our Lodges are Ritual, Masonic knowledge, Dress and Appearance, Conduct, Propriety and the one we want to continue to discuss in this chapter, which is the Masonic Dining experience.

Why we have lost the practice of the Festive Board is anyone's guess. However, we have gone from dining to gulping. We have gone from an after meeting dinner and fellowship gathering with purpose and structure to "Grab a Bite" where Brothers come and go as they please with no structure and no meaning.

We have lost the purpose of the Festive Board of fellowship in a gentlemanly setting, where they can enjoy the social pleasure of dining and where importance is given to both the dinner and its ambience.

There are very few Brothers that know what a Festive Board is or can explain it. Since our Brethren suffer from the lack of wanting to increase their knowledge of Masonry unless they can get it in a sound bite of 30 seconds or less like most information is received in our society today by the populous, the majority of the Brethren cannot understand what all the fuss is about.

Consequently, they grab a bite to eat in a hurry before the

Lodge meeting, run through the meeting as fast as they can and leave without the opportunity to learn about Masonry in the Lodge or the opportunity to dine in fellowship with their Brethren. And you wonder why so many dropped out or feel they did not find what they came here to do.

Although the Festive Board was brought up it was not for the purpose of discussing the actual event, but to discuss its benefits of creating a Masonic dining experience among Brothers for their conviviality and fellowship to reinforce the bonds of Brotherhood.

I recommend every Brother that reads this small section in this book to explore further on all the details of a Festive Board; its history, traditions and actual practices. I further encourage the Brothers to practice this concept within their Lodge. It will help create a better Lodge, bring the Brothers closer and truly form great friendships, thus giving the Brethren an opportunity to get together in a less formal atmosphere where they can get to know one another better and share this wonderful Fraternity we call Freemasonry in an oasis of peace and tranquility, leaving the cares of the world outside the doors and practice true Brotherhood with those that came here to learn to subdue their passions and improve themselves in Masonry.

Chapter 15

Membership

Yes, we can increase our numbers in Masonry,
but we can lose Masonry while we are doing it"
—LaMoine Langston, PGM of New Mexico

It took Masons in America nearly a century to forget the disaster of rapid growth, of indiscriminate expansion, of making unqualified individuals Masons of the early1800's.

Yes, this stain if you will on our Craft basically came a century after four Lodges in London got together to form a central governing body to make and uphold the standards adopted by this new organization called the Grand Lodge of London and Westminster in 1717, which through evolution became the United Grand Lodge of England.

Masonship vs. Membership has been at the root cause of our humble beginnings of Modern Masonry. It has been the cause in America of our greatest setback, and it is the cause of our present situation, which is diminishing our principles, tenets, usages and customs for the sake of an ever-elusive increase in numbers.

We are fighting a three hundred year battle. The difference is that in its third century we are not as close to the source as we once were. We have too few strong knowledgeable characters on the scene with a solid Masonic background and too many people who are focused on the organization and not on the principles that came together to forge the organization that is Modern Masonry today and stand in the way of doing the right thing because they cannot comprehend the difference.

The mentality of "more is better" is something that we continue to struggle with nearly 300 years later and I wonder, and maybe you have too, why do we continue to use the same playbook and expect different results.

Maybe, like me, you wonder why we continue to imitate other social and service clubs when they themselves are suffering from the same situation of lack of membership. And, maybe, like me, you wonder if the decrease in membership is really a problem or not, or just another cyclical event.

Therefore, the debate should be do we change our principles, tenets, usages and customs in order to increase our membership or do we maintain them and learn to do with less, until we set our house on the proper path in order to fulfill our promise, which has been so long neglected by so many.

Our Fraternity has always been very strict or selective on whom we let in. As a matter of fact this is one of the reasons, if not the main reason, why we were assembled into Grand Lodges and Subordinate Lodges—that we may have a central body that would hold the standard of membership in the Particular or Subordinate Lodges.

Yet these same Grand Lodges through their leadership

have changed those same standards, which were the reasons why they were created in the first place. Yet they have not solved the problem (which in my mind is not the problem) they were trying to solve, which was an increase in membership.

So we continue to chop at the symbolic cedar, which is Freemasonry in order to make Masonry more common and acceptable, thereby losing its value, eroding its principles and in the course changing Masonry into another failed Social Club.

All the while we should be standing firm on our principles, tenets, usages and customs, thereby setting a positive contrast between Masonry and other social and service clubs.

There can be no doubt that we have a specific purpose that no other institution has and which we dedicate ourselves to "Making Good Men Better." This is our goal and we need to stay focused. Watering this purpose does not help our cause at all, yet too many leaders are too concerned with the needs of the organization instead of finding ways to uphold and exalt the reasons for its existence.

One example, which is obvious as the day is long, yet the majority of the leadership in America has dedicated the last three quarters of a century to it without success, is membership. Here we have forgotten the famous definition of insanity by Albert Einstein. "Insanity: doing the same thing over and over again and expecting different results." We should be applying this to ourselves when it comes to recruitment of membership regardless of how politically correct you may make the nomenclature, this is the organization overriding the principles.

My Brothers this is the reason why we find ourselves in this situation where years of neglect to duty has lead us to this sense of urgency with membership as if this would fix our problems.

The ego's lack of knowledge, and if it "isn't broke don't fixed it" which is the slogan the status quo group uses to disguise their do nothing efforts, is what drives most of our failures including the reason for our existence of "Making Good Men Better." Self-improvement of the individual character should and must remain our number one goal.

Many in our leadership have forgotten or have never known the main purpose of this Fraternity, so eloquently stated in the following question: "What came you here to do?" The answer to this question and the following question and answer in your catechism is the essence of what we need to do and the reason why you are accepted among the Brethren.

My Brothers, membership is not the problem, it has never been the problem and it can never be the problem because we place no value on quantity of membership but on the quality of the individual member.

An individual who of his own volition seeks to become a member and meets the qualities demanded of all petitioners is accepted to become a member based on his promise of self-improvement and a lifetime dedication to this cause.

Our problem has and will continue to be the leadership's failure to focus the Craft on the task at hand, which is to learn to conquer our emotions and better ourselves in Masonry. This has been our greatest failure as a whole and one that will lead us to destroy Masonry from within. Are there exceptions to the rules? You bet—you and others out there. But we are the minority. We need to speak up and be heard that others may follow. Lead by word but more importantly by example.

This can be accomplished just like it was accomplished nearly three centuries ago.

Below you will find some of the innovations the leadership has made in the body of Masonry. Solutions sold to the Craft as events that would turn around the perceived problem of membership and the Craft's ignorance of the errors about to be committed by changing the principles, tenets, usages and customs have followed blindly, their leaders not thinking nor knowing the grave effects it would reap.

- Ballot Box changes from one ball or cube to reject to multiples as many as three.
- Lowering the standards as to the moral quality and character of the candidate,
- Accepting felonious individuals
- Shortening of catechism if any
- One Day Classes
- No Education requirement and none given at Lodge level

These measures did not only not turn the losing tide in membership, but now we have more Brothers that do not know, understand nor have been taught what Masonry is and in some cases they have been coached to accept some of these solutions when they would have preferred another had they had the opportunity to know the difference or make the choice.

Here I have to say something about one of the poorest tools created to artificially increase Masonic membership—the "One Day Class" which has yet to make even the slightest increase in membership while we have sacrificed many of the usages and customs and let them loose with little information at best and no education in general and expect them to fit in. This has been a failure at best in making

Masons, and brought us an insignificant financial increase. In the most part they have abandoned that which they seek and never found.

This drive-thru mentality can only lead us to doom. Not everything that is big is good and not everything that is fast is good. Masonry my Brothers is a life journey, not a bullet train trip. With commitment, dedication and perseverance you will be able to learn and enjoy your journey in Freemasonry and recognize its value because you have endured a long and rugged road of self-improvement. Perhaps this is the biggest task in your personal life but the most rewarding, because you have continuously faced the man in the mirror and have pushed him to do better each and every single day with the blessings of the Great Architect of the Universe.

How unfortunate for them because our promise was not delivered and today they do not understand what they went through which may lead to a negative impression of our beloved Fraternity, and after all that trouble on both parts they leave us without ever having benefited from their experience.

Remember, quality must never be sacrificed, with no exceptions. Masonry is not for everyone. We are selective. We are looking for a few god men, in order to make an impact in our little corner of the world one man at a time.

I'm a firm believer that we DO NOT have a Membership problem. We have a quality problem and must be more selective with those we allow to join us. Our history has taught us this much. All we need is for the smallest thing to upset the apple cart and we will see a mass exodus from our ranks. It happened in the 1820's with the Morgan Affair and the depression of 1930's where in some states the census dropped by as much as 47% of the membership and it was left to those Masons of quality who stuck through thick and thin under all kinds of adversities and became an even more ardent supporter and spokesman for its great virtues, moral rectitude and unshakeable principles. This is the type of man we need to accept into our numbers and nothing less than the best.

Our system for selection is broken in many Lodges; there is a nonchalant and indifferent type of attitude towards the importance of the Petition's process:

- The character of those being presented as petitioner.
- Of the recommenders who are to eagerly wanting to sign a petition of someone they don't even know.
- The constant recruitment by the same Brothers who seem to bring in all the petitions being presented.
- Of the Petitions & Investigation committees who sometimes even includes the very people who recommend them, a definite conflict of interest.
- A Petitions Committee that doesn't understand their role in the screening process.
- An Investigations Committee which is rubber-stamping these petitions and who in many cases are not known to the Craft because they are not named in open Lodge by the Master.
- Investigations Committee whom are permanently named in the Lodge year after year.
- Investigations Committee who fail to conduct a proper investigation, following up with employer, references, neighbors, and other affiliations the petitioner may have.
- Investigations Committee who do not follow up on information given by petitioner and fail to confirm or deny any allegation.
- Investigations Committee who do a shoddy job and

take as a personal insult if a candidate is rejected.

• Secretaries who conceals information from the Craft that would be pertinent to the possible rejection of the candidate.

• Secretaries who have failed to conduct or conceal the Background Investigation required by some States in order to have the candidate gain acceptance into the Lodge.

• Secretaries who accept and conceal petitions of candidates that do not reside within their jurisdiction and of those that do reside but have not met the proper amount of time.

• Masters too eager to bring in as many petitioners as possible in his year for the sake of boasting that he had the largest number of initiations in his year, yet look around and you will be hard pressed to find anyone of those members in Lodge.

• Masters who manipulate when the petitions will be presented depending on who is present at the Lodge.

• Masters who appoint weak and unknowledgeable Brothers to the Investigation process that he may obtain the results he wishes.

I'm sure I have left some out and again my purpose is not to list all of the cases and faults I have seen and work with but to inform you of the situations that are present in our Lodges.

When conducting an investigation leave no stone unturned and start with questioning the recommenders of their relationship with the petitioner. This will speak volumes of the work you have ahead of you. If you follow your particular Grand Lodge recommendations for conducting a character investigation you will find that it will be a great start. There are also other areas that may assist you with more information to be more proficient in this most important duty of a Master Mason, that of guarding the West Gate. We must adhere to the Ancient Character standards that we may live up to our motto of "Making Good Men Better," or is this just lip service. I know it is not for me, how about you? Get involved and make a difference.

My Brothers, I cannot emphasize enough the importance of making the right choice when it comes to Membership vs. Masonship. This is probably one of your most important duties as a Mason and one that must never be taken lightly should you fail this Venerable Institution and be complicit in its demise.

There must never be a rejection based on the petitioners, race, creed, color, or ethnicity, period. This must never be allowed in Masonry, should Masonry loose its universality, which is one of the greatest assets our institution possesses, where a Mason may find a safe haven anywhere in world.

There must never be a rejection because the petitioner is engaged in the same business as another Brother in the Lodge because of personal reasons, because of his age, young or old, if they possess the qualities and faculties required.

In my mind the only time when there should be a rejection is if the petitioner fails to meet the high standard of quality that must be required of all petitioners, or he is coming with mercenary intents against the Craft. And last but not least, will he be a burden or an asset to the Institution?

Forget the numbers. Quantity has never been important when you are dealing with men and character, when you are looking for excellence, when you are seeking the best of the best. You can accomplish more with a few good men than with a horde of uncaring individuals.

Quality my Brothers is paramount. Remember, you need a Brother that you can trust with the care of your family's wellbeing, finances, and securities that none of them will be disturbed or molested. Does that petitioner possess these qualities? When in doubt vote for the benefit of the Fraternity?

As we have said before, Masonry should be selective in its membership for the reasons discussed previously. However, there are too many in our Institution that see quantity membership as power. More members, lower cost to members and more power with funds. They look at everything as if we were selling a product that was tangible, where if we were in the business of selling eggs the more dozens we produce the more we can sell, the more we sell the more competitive we can become in the market, the greater the market share the more money we make—great business pattern. However, Masonry is not in the egg business and as a matter of fact a few bad eggs metaphorically speaking have given us the greatest stains and shame in the local, national, and international community.

Don't fall for those that tell you that you can have quantity and quality—this is an oxymoron. We must select one or the other. If we choose the first we will continue to struggle in a valueless and meaningless world, and in the antithesis of Freemasonry whose purpose is to take the individual good man and teach him through ritual, lessons, lectures and mentoring to improve himself in Masonry fitting his mind as a living stone for that house not made with hands eternal in the heavens. Perfection and nothing less, my Brothers, that is our solution to membership, don't settle for less.

When it comes to membership we must all be vigilant that the process is seamless with every aspect of it followed in our Lodges and no one is favored or un-favored in this important process, no exceptions.

When it comes to our leadership make sure you elect Brothers that want to maintain our principles, tenets, usages and customs pure and unimpaired. The way to do this is by questioning in detail those who seek to be your future leader and by looking into their previous history and comments, leopards never change their spots and neither do humans.

We must be perseverant, dedicated and committed to Freemasonry and we must be committed to sharing these thoughts with our Brothers for Masonic Education, or for the Good of the Order in our Lodges, by creating study groups and discussing the present condition of our institution and how we need to convey this message to those who seek to lead us.

If you do not expect anything from those who you are bringing in and from those that you are electing to lead, then you will get nothing in return. Expect more from everyone from the lowest Entered Apprentice to the Grand Master, but more importantly, you cannot expect more from them than you expect from yourself.

So what do we need to do to better our membership or Masonship as I prefer to call it? It all starts with you. When you have achieved your goal or master self-improvement and can be an example to others; then start the process of communicating these facts to those that you come in contact with in the course of performing your Masonic duties and don't stop until the battle of quality vs. quantity has been won.

In closing this chapter I want to leave you with the opening quote of this chapter by M∴W∴ LaMoine Langston Past

Grand Master of New Mexico who very wisely warned us when he said **"Yes, we can increase our numbers in Masonry, but we can lose Masonry while we are doing it."** Wiser words were never spoken. It is up to you. Think about it.

Chapter 16

Unqualified Leadership

"There is nothing wrong with your Lodge, nor with Freemasonry, that good leadership will not cure."
—Dwight L. Smith, PGM& PGS Grand Lodge of Indiana

Selecting your leadership should be more than a popularity contest. Selecting a Brother based on who he is a friend of, who he sits with, or whether or not he has served in the previous chair are not good reasons for selecting a Brother. This can be a life and death decision for the Fraternity; we cannot continue to have unqualified leadership without paying a heavy price for it.

In some jurisdictions the average leadership in the Lodges is between six months to 2.5 years as a Master Mason and with almost nonexistent knowledge of Masonic Laws, Rules and Regulations with a great majority of these Brothers not even owning much less reading the Constitution, the Ancient Charges, Landmarks, or Andersons' Constitution nor having a copy of their own Lodge By-laws. How and what can they lead?

Some don't stop there, with a great number of District Deputy Grand Masters having been an average of 1 to 2 years out of the Master's Chair and influencing others with their very limited experiences, and some probably have not even creased the spine of, or peeled the cellophane of the pages of the books mentioned above.

Look at your Lodge and Grand Lodge Officers and you can see that you have Brothers in stations who do not know what is expected of them. They are not prepared to deal with the present responsibilities much less future ones and do not have designs or detail plans on their Trestle Board and in some cases, they not only don't have a rough sketch, they don't have a Trestle Board period. If you have Officers who have nothing, it is your duty and the duty of your fellow members to do better and urge the Brothers in charge to step up or step out. The Craft must assist them in one way or another and encourage them to do the right thing by the Lodge or Grand Lodge as all Masons must.

Earning your support has to be more than a glad hand, a pat on the back, or letting someone else make the decision for you, whether at the Lodge or Grand Lodge. Speaking of making your decision, we have all seen and heard as an annual occurrence at our Lodges, new faces on the night of elections asking other members who to vote for. They have not been in Lodge the whole year and now because they feel they have to be there they have been called by someone to be there, or asked by someone to vote for one particular person and they don't know who to vote for the other positions and ask for guidance.

What the Brother asking may not realize is that the Brother he is asking may have an agenda contrary to what he may believe and not realize that until much later, when the damage done is irreversible.

It is important for the Brothers to come to the Lodge on a regular basis to see if those responsible for the welfare of the Lodge are committed and dedicated to its wellbeing. Are they fulfilling their responsibilities and doing their job according to the rules and regulations they swore to uphold at the time of their installation?

Only regular attendance can give you the insight to these matters. Remember that there is NO regulation that requires for a Brother to be promoted if he doesn't have what it takes or has not performed his previous job in a satisfactory manner. Although promotions are regularly carried out by either the newly elected Worshipful Master in his appointments because he doesn't want to be the bad guy and replace a Brother that has not completed his duties the previous year or by the Craft when after years of underserved promotions by previous Masters, a Brother has reached the place where his next step is election to the Junior Warden Station and the Brethren of the Lodge fail to vote for the benefit of the Lodge and promote yet another undeserving Brother who will in two more years be the Worshipful Master elect, making him another unqualified leader.

If you have an individual at work whose hallmark has been his lack of responsibility, dedication, and commitment to perform the task at hand and you were responsible for promotions in your place of employment; would you promote this individual? The answer will most likely be a resounding NO. The Lodge is no different. Remember that if the Brother has not performed to the best of his ability he does not need to be promoted period. NO SOCIAL PROMOTION. Our system is based on merits and beliefs that only those that apply themselves should be rewarded. DO NOT send the wrong message by rewarding mediocrity, irresponsibility, incompetence, and lack of commitment or dedication.

You may know or recognize what I'm about to write. Because of many years of poor leadership there are many Lodges that have been dead for some years. The only problem is they don't realize it. Simply because they have been operating in this fashion for so long, they don't know any difference. However, anyone else looking in can see that they have been dead for years.

Not because their number has not increased and not because they have not performed a Degree, but simply because they have failed to practice Masonry so many years back. They cannot pinpoint when it stopped being a Masonic Lodge and became a place for social gathering.

The best way to judge a Lodge's performance would be if the Lodge can meet the requirements needed to qualify for a Charter. If it's not, then the Lodge is in trouble and needs to start addressing the situation. This will require solid leadership, first to recognize the problem and secondly to be able to make plans to turn it around. Making Masons requires dedication, commitment and fortitude to teach them how to improve themselves in Masonry.

Leadership skills are what separates the Craft Mason from the Mason who is a Social Clubber. A Masonic Leader knows that Masonry is like no other Fraternity, service or social club and understands the demands of a Masonic Lodge are far beyond any other, because Masonry is here to build character, to teach a man to be become better, one man at a time. Who in turn will influence those closest to him by making his corner of the world much better for all concerned?

Some of the qualifications for making a good Masonic Leader are:

- Good and punctual attendance.
- Proper attire to meetings (depending on Lodge minimum coat and tie)
- Participation within the Lodge committees, ritual and Degrees.
- Willingness to assist and teach others who are in positions or places under his care.
- Has taken Masonic Educational Courses available to him in his own jurisdiction or from the MSA to let him know more about his duties as an Officer or Master of the Lodge.
- Has copy of his Lodge By-Laws and understands them.
- Owns and uses his Ahiman Rezon. (Book of Constitution)
- Follows the rules and leads by example.
- Able to plan and execute on such plans.
- Gets others involved.
- Teaches others to lead.
- Courteous, kind and caring.
- Provides an ambience for learning and fellowship.
- Makes sure that Entered Apprentice, Fellow Craft and Master Masons feel welcome, highlighting Brotherly Love and Affection as well as mentoring and ritual instruction.
- Promotes fellowship in every instance.
- Is he Responsible, Dedicated, and Committed to Masonry?

I'm sure you will have others to add to the list above, however it is not the intent of the author to list them all, but to give you an overview to help you think and expand on your own requirements and make your own list that would apply to yourself and those you select for leadership wherever and whenever you have this responsibility. We can make a difference in our Lodges and Grand Lodges if we do a better job in the selection process by applying the requirements we may expect from those who seek to lead us in the future. My Brothers it is time we break away from the status quo.

Although status quo may be a comfortable place for many, it has never been a place where a Craft Mason would want to or should be, because this would be the antithesis to our goals of "Making good men better." Also, status quo would mean there would be no requirement for self-improvement or transformation of a neophyte into a Mason, of a good man into a better man. Which is not what Masonry's goal has been for nearly 300 years of modern history. Masonry is a way of life; a life of dedication, commitment, and perseverance to attain that which we know cannot be attained in this world.

Let us not settle for the status quo. Rock the boat, expect better, and demand more not only from those who lead, but also from ourselves. Get involved, step up and become the dedicated Mason who would do whatever it takes for Masonry to succeed in your Lodge and Grand Lodge as long as it meets with our rules and regulations, but more importantly with your particular Sacred Volume of Law which is always the best guide in doing things right.

Unqualified Leadership leads to a spiraling effect of settling for less and less qualified leaders. If the bar is not raised, you will continue to go down the slippery road of having more unqualified individuals seeking positions of leadership. After all there is nothing to it! Look at what was achieved by the predecessors in your Lodge or Grand Lodge—nothing. As one Mason put it, which at the time took many by surprise and I quote, "They are only there for the Big Apron and Collar." Unfortunately this has come to be more truthful than we care to acknowledge.

Look at your Institution. Do a self-analysis and be truthful. Ask is Freemasonry better today than yesterday, or the year before or the one before that, and have your leaders improved or lessened the values of Freemasonry. Are they making Masons or members? Is the focus on the number of Masons or the quality of Masons? Don't be fooled by slogans that proclaim you can have both, quantity and quality— that would be an oxymoron. If that weren't the case then why lower the standards for gaining acceptance into the Greatest Fraternity known to man.

Challenge yourself to make the right choices for you, your Lodge and your Grand Lodge based on sound information, research, and by asking the pertinent questions of those who would lead you. Become involved. Don't settle for less than excellence; make the right choice, choose for Freemasonry. You owe it to yourself and the near 300 year legacy of modern Freemasonry. Celebrate our next centennial with a real pledge on your part of dedication, commitment and responsibility expected from an Accepted Mason.

I find Master Masons most interesting. They have all gone through the Fellow Craft Degree which is the representation of manhood in the preparation of life with a wide and varied education as represented in the lecture explaining the different senses of the human body with which to learn and the five orders of architecture with which to build and the seven liberal arts with which to expand your knowledge of all things surrounding you and for the individual growth to make a good man better. We, more often than not, fail to see the lesson of this. What did we come here to do? We came to learn to improve ourselves in Masonry in order to become an Accepted Mason. Do you fit the definition of an Accepted Mason? This is for you to answer.

Next time you attend an election remember that if you have inadequate and un-qualified leadership you have no one to blame but yourself. Get engaged, and assist those around you to do the same. Our Fraternity's future rests on our ability to weed out the weak and unqualified leader. Are you ready? Freemasonry needs YOU. Do your part.

Give us a chance to succeed by selecting the best Brother for the job, based on real facts, in-depth study, and asking the right questions. Make the future brighter by selecting qualified leaders.

Chapter 17

Leadership

"Leaders aren't born they are made, and they are made just like anything else, through hard work and that's the price we have to pay to achieve that goal or any goal."
—*Vince Lombardi*

Leaders are made through hard work, dedication, commitment and sacrifice, by accepting the responsibilities which come with whatever commitment he has given his word to, simply because a Mason's word is his bond and his actions will be measured by the square, level and plumb in all his undertakings. Although we are bound by our many obligations, nonetheless you should expect the Mason to do the right thing because he is a Mason, above all.

My experience is that many of those who I have met who have sought leadership positions in their Lodges or Grand Lodges have done so because this is the next step or title to seek for the sake of the title and not because they have a plan to lead. A plan has not been expected nor has anyone questioned it before. Why should they even bother with having a plan? You will probably give or beg him to take the job and the qualifications don't matter to you, as long as you don't have anything to do. This is not leadership from those who seek to lead or those that are being led.

Looking at the previous statement, would you trust an individual or your child to take over your business or household without him being instructed or well-schooled on how to run the operation, the important and the not so important aspects of the business, the need to be punctual and to conduct themselves with the highest and upmost honesty and commitment to the task at hand? Would you leave him in charge of all your worldly possessions and the wellbeing of your company or household for an entire year without constant supervision? The most logical answer will be a resounding NO. Guess what, we do it in Masonry and moreover we say he is in total control without restraints except those within the Laws of which he is not aware of because he has not obtained a copy of the laws much less become acquainted with them, in many cases.

Since leadership must depend on knowledge of whatever the field may be in order to be successful it is that we find ourselves wandering in the wilderness of despair because the organization has become greater than its founding principles. As a result we no longer practice those principles. We are too concentrated on maintaining the organization and our leaders do not know nor do they understand the difference.

From my perspective there are three types of leadership. The "go at it alone" and they will be the savior of our Fraternity single-handedly and that on them will be bestowed the glory of its salvation. Secondly, the "status quo" type, who does not do anything and runs away from any decision-making. The minute they get in they start the countdown to when they will be out, and give explicit instructions to their subordinates to avoid any controversy or unpleasantness at any cost. And the third is the type who wants to work and build a consensus but finds that no one wants to commit to anything from the status quo group or the other who is chomping at the bit to be the savior all on his own.

So, what should we be expecting or demanding from our future leaders whether at Lodge or Grand Lodge? We expect nothing less than excellence and a willingness to be a servant of the Craft and not the Craft as their servant. We must expect a plan, a vision for the future that will lead us to greater heights. We must have discussions on how the plan will be implemented, paid for, affect our long-term stability, and make certain it does not change Freemasonry as we know it.

We should vote not based on what appointment we may receive, but for the greater good of our Fraternity. Not on whom they know, but what they know. We must expect knowledge of the Law and our history; we must expect dedication, commitment and sacrifice to the Masonic Principles by their word that these will not be altered or amended. We must demand that they work together for the benefit of our Fraternity. We cannot continue to reinvent the wheel every single year, or tolerate those that do nothing but just coast for however long the Lodge or Grand Lodge line may be, knowing that all that needs to be done is to get elected to the bottom of the line and coast for however long is needed to reach the top. We must be so ever vigilant that the right Brother receives the rewards of leadership; otherwise we are doomed to failure for yet another year.

We need leaders that ask for our opinion and seek our

input, but not when they are Worshipful Master or Grand Master because by then it is too late; their groundwork should have been laid down long before with proper designs upon the Trestle Board for us to follow. This is nothing but fluff with no substance, and 'make you feel good' politics to make you think you matter. When was the last time any of the suggestions given saw the meridian light, but at the end of the day we have not moved our Fraternity forward yet another year. We cannot continue to afford this year after year. Something has to give and I'm afraid it will be our Fraternity. If you don't believe it look around you.

As the legend teaches us, when there were no designs upon the Trestle Board confusion was created among the Craft. The Craft has had no designs upon the Trestle Board for many years (with few exceptions). If you know anything about construction, in order to build something magnificent and spectacular you need full and detailed plans, not rough sketches. We need true Craftsman and Master Overseers to step up to the plate and lay down true and square work upon the Trestle Board for the Craft to follow. Anything short of full and detailed plans will lead to anything else but a magnificent and spectacular building.

Of course the magnificent and spectacular building we are speaking about is Freemasonry, and like in any building the structure cannot be compromised. The pillars which support our institution of Wisdom, Strength, and Beauty must rest upon a solid foundation of the Principle Tenants of our Fraternity which must never be altered or changed save we change the meaning of Freemasonry forever.

So, where does your next leader stand on these principles? Has he stipulated, or have you asked what his record is and what are his qualifications? Is he capable of designing full and detailed plans for a brighter horizons and a new dawn of prosperity for the Craft—not because his designs can increase the membership number but because he has made Masons by following the principles in the Masonic blueprint laid down from time immemorial. A blueprint that bases his designs on true Masonic Principles making good men better one individual at a time with proper mentoring and education, laying the road to success.

Masonic leadership is in all of us whether you believe or not. You took initiative to seek and you found out who and what we were. Initiative is a leadership quality. You followed it up by asking of your own free will and accord and you knocked on our door and it was opened unto you. This demonstrated commitment (another leadership quality), and you asked and it was given unto you. You asked—another leadership quality—that of recognizing you needed assistance to accomplish your goals.

Now, a new door has been opened for you. A new chapter in your life has been opened as well and now it is required of you that you follow up on your promise of: "What came you here to do?" The answer: "To learn to subdue my passions and improve myself in Masonry." Your commitment to improve yourself is another measure of your leadership and one that only you can answer. Have you improved yourself in Masonry inwardly and outwardly? Have you built on the leadership qualities you used to get this far? If not, why not? As a Mason you are on a search for light, and following the lessons of your Degrees identifying your three stages of life you need to use well that second stage of learning and expand your horizons well, as Masonry is a lifelong career of self-improvement until perfection is reached in our last stage when we begin a perfect life in Thy Lodge on High.

As you can see we are all called to be leaders as we work on our self to improve as human beings for our betterment and, in turn, those around us. It is our duty to serve our Fraternity in whatever place we can qualify depending on our leadership skills and not based on vanity or greed; not to be served but to be a servant and these are the qualifications we should be looking for in those that want to lead, including ourselves. We should all be measured by the same standards. There should never be any social promotions for leadership; only those with the best qualities, only those that have been tried and willing to be tried again. Those are the things leaders are made of, are you? And more importantly is the Brother or Brothers seeking the leadership role made up of the qualities needed or are they filled with egotism and vanity.

We all have a duty as Masons to serve our Brothers if we have the qualities necessary for whatever the position or level we seek to serve. This is our duty, plain and simple, nothing personal. If those making the decision find us qualified to serve then we should gladly step up and take the responsibility, if not we should gladly step back and work with those that have been accepted and fill our roll wherever we can do the best work.

So what shall we expect from the Brothers seeking to be our leaders and run the operations of our Lodge and Grand Lodge and be qualified to design full and detailed plans on the Trestle Board, which can deliver a better tomorrow for our Fraternity.

- Knowledge and understanding of the Ahiman Rezon or Masonic Law of your Jurisdiction.
- Knowledge of the By-laws of the Lodges in your Jurisdiction.

- Understand and completed the Masonic Education material/MSA educational material.
- Understand and completed Masonic Leadership material/MSA educational material.
- Has he achieved **results** in his previous stations, and committee assignments, it is not how many committees he has served but what has he accomplished during his time of service.
- Look at the resumes and investigate from those he served with, how had he performed his committee duties, you will be amazed at what you will find. Many Brothers have impressive resumes because they have committed to travel or are popular but have never performed their duties; our organization is replete with folks like this. Also, look at the reports of your Grand Lodge proceedings to see some of the fruits of his labors in the committee reports.
- Ask his fellow District Deputies, Past and current Masters of his Lodge about his conduct and performance.
- An understanding of Business operations, and responsibilities of being in charge.
- An understanding that he is being elected to serve as the Worshipful Master or Grand Master of Masons and shall at all times represent Masonry's interest first.
- That he will not violate and/or ignore the Principles that founded this organization as others have already done in some jurisdictions.
- Ask any and all pertinent questions respectfully as long as they are related to Masonry, with no personal attacks, hidden agendas and always focus on what is best for Masonry.
- Ask about quality verses quantity. Is he for rushing members through?

- Ask him to tell you the responsibilities for the positions he is going to hold office if elected.
- Ask him if he will apply the law equally or favor his friends.
- Ask him about his vision for Freemasonry; see if it's comparable with your vision for a better tomorrow. But more importantly ask him for details—that is where the devil always resides. Blanket sweeping statements or fancy talking points cannot make up the need to know what this Brother will commit our Fraternity too when he is in charge.

A leader will be able to work and fulfill every single question you ask and he should understand that his answer will make a difference in his future.

Better yet, it is my firm belief that unless someone in the Lodge or forum is ready to write all questions and answers asked of one candidate so the same may be asked of the next candidate. Better all candidates should be there at the same time alternating the questions so that everything is equal. After all, these Masons are our Brothers. Whether we vote for them or not based on their qualifications and visions is a separate issue. However, they should all be treated with the same courtesy and respect all Master Masons deserve from one to another.

If you have Officers who are doing the right thing make sure you praise and work with them. You have the exception to the rule and should not hesitate to participate and dedicate yourself to see the Officers and Lodge continue to move forward.

The lesson to learn here is to be careful whom you select to lead, whether in Lodge or Grand Lodge. Nothing is guaranteed to anyone. Do your homework. Vote for what you believe is the better choice based on research and questioning of the candidates. DO NOT give your vote away to anyone for frivolous reasons. Do not be lazy. The wellbeing of your Lodge and Grand Lodge depends on you performing your Masonic duties.

Chapter 18

What Of Our Posterity?

"And may the tenets of our profession be transmitted through your Lodge, pure and unimpaired, from generation to generation."
—Masonic Monitor

Our Fraternity, like our nations democracy, is always one generation away from extinction and this is not a bad thing at all because it allows all of those involved to buy in and demonstrate their due diligence in accepting such an awesome responsibility—that it does not perish under their watch.

Will we fail in our watch? This is a question that we must all answer and one that must always be present on our minds if we are to profoundly affect our posterity?

We were blessed to have received the gift of a great Fraternity and during the course of our Masonic life, which will stretch for several generations. We must look at every step of the way on our long Masonic career to insure that our great Fraternity is delivered to our posterity in better shape than it was handed to us.

As a reminder of this commitment let me quote you two small parts of our Installation Ceremonies, in the beginning, "They were entrusted in peace and honor to the Masons of ancient times, and have been faithfully transmitted to us, it is our duty to convey them unimpaired to the latest posterity." And at the end: "And may the tenets of our profession be transmitted through your Lodge, pure and unimpaired, from generation to generation."

The first portion was as an explanation of the duties and responsibilities of Masons and the end is part of the Charge given all the Brethren to live and act by.

This assurance is what I would like to address both on the institutional and financial side of our Fraternity. Are we doing everything according to the tenets and principles of our Fraternity so that when the time comes we leave this Fraternity unimpaired and full of glory?

Regarding our institutional side of this commitment, are we communicating the principles of Masonry through your Lodge unadulterated and unhindered, to future generations?

This to me is the greatest risk our Fraternity has encountered on a constant basis in the last three to four decades, which began possibly as much as three to four decades earlier. This is mostly due to poor education, lack of reflection, and failure to understand the importance of our predecessors work when it comes to the concept, limitations and standards set to separate Freemasonry from everything else known to mankind at that time.

This constant barrage has led to innovations on the body of Masonry which were introduced for one purpose only and it usually is addressing the increase of numbers in membership. Regardless of how wrong this is, it continues to drive the leadership to new lows in spite of the damage it may perpetuate on this Noble and Venerable Fraternity.

The great thing is that our Fraternity is not national and therefore you hear of an innovation in one state or another that affects that entire State population but not the whole country.

The innovations that have changed the Fraternity, even if it's only one or two Grand Lodges, have been:

• Ballot Box changes from one ball or cube to reject to multiples as many as three.

• Lowering the standards as to the moral quality and character of the candidate, by accepting individuals who would not have been proposed two or three decades ago.

• One Day Classes.

Other changes that do not help Freemasonry in any way possible but are being implemented are:

• Poor results from the Investigation Committees, through ignorance or willful disregard of their duties.

• Shortening of catechism, if any.

• No Education requirement and none given at Lodge level.

However, these accomplished some discord in Lodges where Candidates were rejected by members of the Lodge and yet initiated because they now needed to have more than one rejection, disrupting the harmony of the Lodge. It did accomplish bringing in Candidates that were not the best representation of what a Mason should be. It did accomplish the dumbing-down of Freemasonry by eliminating or limiting the Candidates exposure to the required education before and during the Degrees. These changes have not achieved what they were intended to accomplish, which was a turnaround in the decline of membership. But they have dimmed the bright Light of Masonry in these places a little bit.

Our leadership needs to understand that we need to leave our posterity an educated Craft or they would be destined to fail.

The other threat to our posterity's future is the financial side of our Fraternity. Here in the majority of the cases we inherited properties and financial stability and in the majority of the cases the Brethren are living on what their predecessors left them and have not paid their way.

Even more distressing is the fact that the properties inherited, regardless of their shape in the majority of the cases, have not been improved but actually allowed to be rundown to the point where many edifices have become an embarrassment to have the Masonic name or Square and Compass upon the building.

Here, to the credit of some Grand Lodges, their Constitutions allow them to make decisions as to whether or not some Lodges will have joint residency of one building, closing others and bringing the one building into something fitting of our Craft and the neighborhood it resides in.

In visiting Lodges in and out of my jurisdiction or in my travels I see Lodges from the road and I must honestly say that many leave a lot to be desired. You can tell that sometime ago these building were pretty much the crème of the crop in those communities, but now the years of neglect have taken a toll on them. Unfortunately we can't see the forest for the trees as we are so use to these surroundings that we do not notice the deterioration or deplorable conditions of the physical building, inside and out.

Here again is one of these things that directly or indirectly will have an effect on membership. The simple fact is, who would want to belong to something that does not care for their property and allows it to be so run down that it becomes an embarrassment to the community in which it resides?

Our buildings are the windows to the soul of Freemasonry in the communities in which they reside and speak volumes of the type of individuals that belong to it by the physical appearance of these structures.

The disrepair is so extensive in some Lodges that it would be virtually impossible to correct the problems in a cost effective way, yet the Brethren there can't see it and will not do anything to change it. It would be better if this building is shut down and the proceeds from it put to better use and they rent or buy a new location for their meeting.

The attachments to material things for nostalgic reasons are not the thinking of a Mason who should be practical, prudent and knowledgeable enough to make the decision of what is best for the Craft as a whole and not for individual or selfish reasons.

Finally, the real reason behind the majority of these cases is the money. Always follow the money and you will find the root cause of the problem, whether it is from the lack of or the misuse of funds. Both point to the irresponsibility of the members of that Particular Lodge to see the importance to not only pay their proper share but to leave to posterity something they can be proud of.

Don't leave your future generations a burden, leave them a legacy of commitment, dedication, and sacrifice which will be readily seen by the way your Lodge looks in and out and the financial stability of the same. Not necessarily because they have thousands of dollars in the bank (although this would be great) but by the fact that the members of the Lodge are paying their fair share and maintaining the Lodge in good repair in and out; a place where Brothers will find a warm and welcoming environment.

This will make it a place where your members would want to attend and a place where they will feel comfortable bringing in their peers and possible members. Not to mention when you bring the Ladies and family to a dinner or open ceremonies, they will let you know how they really feel about going to your Lodge, the conditions of the kitchen and bathrooms, the clutter about the different rooms and the dust and spider webs all over the place. They will let you know if this is a warm place or a cold dark dungeon filled with critters and smells.

The financial stability of our Fraternity is something that concerns me a great deal, especially when I discovered that there were some Lodges where dues were as low as $15.00 annually including per capita, which was $14.00. You will probably think these figures could not be right, but I assure you they are correct and truthful.

This Particular Lodge had an increase in dues 1954 when they raised their dues to $11.00 and stayed at the same rate until 2004 when they were raised to $15.00 until 2012. If you figure for inflation, this Lodge's dues should have been a minimum of $77.25 in 2004 and $93.89 in 2012, just to keep up with inflation, not considering the buying power of the dollar which has diminished considerably. (Side note: this Lodge did increase their dues in 2012 to $60.00)

As an example of the buying power of the dollar and the way that things have increased during this same period of time we can look at the cost of electricity. There was an increase of 3.4% from January of 1959 to January of 1969, compared with a 4.4% increase from January 2013 to January 2014.

Looking at the same report, the average electrical bill in 1954 was $30.00 plus dollars for a household, and today the same house would be $207.36. Of course, there are many more examples of the increase of cost and the diminishing purchasing power of the dollar.

In this Lodge, like in many others, there are those Brothers whose benevolence knows no bounds and they step up to the plate and carry an unfair burden of the Lodge expenses. Whether they can afford it or not is not the question. The question here is really one that is simple and addresses the quality of the membership. Are you a freeloader or NOT?

It seems that in today's society being a freeloader, deadbeat, or moocher brings no social stigma. However, for a Mason this is not acceptable. A Mason pays his way; he seeks no charity for himself but for others. He is benevolent to a fault. He would never consider taking from anyone more especially taking from or strapping undue burden on future generations, regardless of how acceptable this practice may be in today's society. A Mason does not live by what may be socially acceptable but by a Moral Compass, which is guided by his faith and practice of the same. We are a notch above the rest.

It is necessary for the Lodge leadership to be aware of these two situations in their Lodge and take immediate action to correct the institutional and financial problems; and both start with Education.

I firmly believe that the majority of the Craft will do the right thing by their Fraternity when confronted with it and given the facts and where they are allowed to make a decision without pressure or coercion from those in the leadership position.

If we are going to have a future and if that future is going to be that of a rising sun, instead of a setting sun, we need to be proactive in straightening out our current deficiencies by being strong proponents of keeping the Masonic Principles intact and keeping up-to-date with our financial responsibilities by visiting the values and cost of operating the Lodge on a yearly basis. (Cost of operations is all expenses regardless of how small, divided by the current membership, including cost for capital improvements).

The reality is that many Lodges do not have a clear understanding of how much it costs to keep their doors open. Tracking the expenses for the previous year and making a budget would certainly go a long way to insure the savings, if any, or to insure that the benevolence of a Brother(s) is not abused by the majority of the Lodge.

Once the real figures are known, then the membership should adjust their dues accordingly to include all the expenses of the Lodge, including capital improvements and any other event they may wish to have since they will be paying for it, not limited to a percentage of the budget to be deposited in the savings for future generations, should it be required of them.

Chapter 19

Are We Listening?

"Hypocrisy can afford to be magnificent in its promises, for never intending to go beyond promise, it costs nothing."
—*Edmund Burke*

Have you stopped to wonder what was really meant by this or are you so desensitized that you do not even hear the words or even worse, listen to their meaning? After all, they were intended to deliver a message. Are you listening?

It seems to me that the more information we have available, the less we use. Why, you may wonder! You may be the exception to this statement since you are reading to expand your horizons. It seems sometimes they may be suffering from information overload because they do not like to read or research and are accustomed to sound bites and talking points being their entire source of information. Everything else, like your mom used to say, simply goes in one ear and out the other, without any retention.

All too often we recite things in a parrot like manner

without listening to the words being recited and although at one time they might have had some meaning we have repeated them so much that we no longer remember the meaning nor the reason why it was important for it to be recited.

The more things are made common the more value they lose, for as humans we take common things for granted. Our Fraternity is a perfect example of this phenomenon and one that some very prudent, knowledgeable, and prominent Masons warned us of a couple of hundred years ago.

One of these Brothers was none other than Rev. Dr. George Oliver, a great Masonic scholar of the 19th Century, who said in his Selected Aphorisms number LXIX. "Be very cautious whom you recommend as a Candidate for Initiation: one false step on this part may be fatal. If you introduce a disputatious person, confusion will be produced, which may end in the dissolution of the Lodge, you have a good Lodge, keep it select. Great numbers are not always beneficial." Many Masonic Scholars have said it just as eloquently before and after him, because there is so much truth in this statement for Masonry and most things in life.

Important things taken for granted will prove to weaken and destroy that which was considered important and be detrimental to the survival of the individual, Lodge or Institution. This is true in our personal lives, our Fraternal Institutions and the country in which you may reside.

Total commitment on our part to stop taking things for granted as individuals in our personal lives, Institutions and Nation is the only way we can turn things around.

So let us start by listening to ourselves and to the reasons why we became Masons. Are we here because we were curiosity seekers or are we here because we wanted to be a part of this organization since the people we thought of as our mentors were Masons or are we here because of its rich history?

Whatever the reason, I hope that you have remained because you found something in it that was worth belonging to and although you may not have taken full advantage of it, you can see where we can all do better if we just simply start listening to its core principles, constitutions, rules and regulations and most importantly to the lessons taught in its Rituals.

No longer take for granted those words recited so often at our Degrees. Whether it is the Obligations, Lectures, or Charges, they all have meaning and the lessons are of great value. I ask you if you are delivering them, do it with emphasis. Deliver the story with heartfelt feelings and if you are listening hang on to every word and give it time to sink in and reflect on the message they are conveying to you personally and to the Craft as a whole.

Stop hearing and start listening or if necessary do as your mom used to tell you. Put one finger in your ear so that things don't run out as they ran in, figuratively. We need to slow down enough to be able to absorb what we are supposed to be paying attention to, so we may benefit from its moral lessons. Simply it will take what it takes, depending on your ability to assimilate the information. Never cut yourself short. I often see people trying to cut corners in order to save time and who don't deliver a message, wasting the time of those that participated, however little it was. This I have seen also as an excuse because there is no message to deliver; yet they were in leadership positions and had nothing to say.

My Brothers, although our discourse in today's society is one in which words tend to not have meaning, they do, and although our society is much more impersonal than previous ones, it doesn't mean we have to participate in such behavior.

Words have meaning and consequences.

The challenge for you and me is to begin the slow process of retraining our minds and consciences to start to listen and to further absorb the information. Through this process and only this process can we turn around this epidemic of ignorance.

What a wonderful experience it would be for the Brothers to listen to the Rituals and learn the lessons taught in them, and by the obligations, charges and lessons taught in the lectures of all Three Degrees, which are in effect from the very moment we made them our own; one not replacing the other but complimenting each other and all three in effect for as long as we are in this imperfect world.

What a wonderful world it would be if we can influence our little part of the world by practicing those lessons with our families, in our place of work, our place of worship and in our communities in general.

This is the way that Ancient Craft Masonry intended to better the world by "making good men better" one man at a time and in turn he would influence his corner of the world by his way of life—one that would be worthy of emulation by others.

Now it is left up to each and every one of us that is truly interested in making a difference in our lives, in our Craft, in our Lodges, and in our communities to put on our listening ears and heed the lessons that are being imparted to us every time we attend our Lodges, practice our Ritual or read our laws.

So let us do like the Ritual says. Practice out of the Lodge those great moral lessons taught in it, that the world would recognize the great love Masonry has for humanity in general and the Masons in particular. Are you listening?

Chapter 20

Taking Care Of Business

"You can delegate authority, but not responsibility."
—*Stephen W. Comiskey*

After practicing Masonry in and out of the Lodge for more than 30 years and having been an Officer in the Lodge, District and Grand Lodge and all of the travels of not only my state but many other states in the United States and abroad, I believe our Fraternity is going in the wrong direction.

The sad part of it is that very knowledgeable Masons warned us of the pitfalls the future held for us. Unfortunately, what we have done is we have ignored the facts as presented by many and tried to reinvent Freemasonry or you can say "the wheel" by short timers that were not very well versed in Masonry, whom in the name of leaving a legacy have chopped at the Masonic Pine leaving it weaker in every instance which can ultimately destroy Masonry as we know it.

Thank God for good or bad that we do not have a National

Body per se or we may have even greater troubles than we presently have. As it stands, not all mistakes are being made at the same time in every Jurisdiction. However, one thing that continues to hurt us greatly in my perspective is that the majority of the Jurisdictions do not have long-term plans or goals because of the nature of our structure. This can also be said of the Lodges as well where no sooner one Officer leaves that the other works just as hard not to build on the previous year but erase if he can everything that was achieved.

Secondly, the majority of the Jurisdictions operate on a status quo basis where the Fraternity or Fraternal side is much ignored in action, although it does get an honorable mention here and there but for the most part it is lip service. Again this can also be applied to the Lodges where the Master does very little if anything to educate and promote Masonry, but is too busy in Degrees that are not well performed so they can boast they brought so many members instead of being able to boast about how many they retained, how many they brought back, how many they have helped to fulfill their Masonic dreams, and how many Masons they MADE.

I find that many of the Brethren in leadership positions do very little to expand their horizons, like reading and studying the reports generated in their Jurisdictions thereby ignoring the problems the Craft is confronting at the local level. And the Lodge at the local level is too busy complaining about the Grand Lodge requirements instead of doing something positive by demonstrating their willingness to complete the task at hand like many others have done and become the better for it. Why can't everyone else?

Becoming a Grand Lodge Officer can take you away from the Craft if you let it. Especially by those who use being such an Officer as an excuse of how busy they are and do not participate with the Craft as a regular Brother to see what is really going on. This is a paradox. They seek you out for your support in order to get elected and afterwards, like a typical politician, they don't have any time for you.

Funny enough, they will tell you how busy they are to do anything, and I challenge you to see what they have done at the end of their term and you will probably find out that they did much of nothing on the average. Here again this is the same in most Lodges. The Masters are batting about with much action of total inaction. In other words, much to do about nothing because at the end of the year that Craft that was under his care is not much better at all. If you are the exception congratulations, you kept your promise, as Masons are required to do.

Becoming a Grand Lodge Officer and eventually Grand Master is looked at as the obvious next step in their Masonic career because when you looked at what the holders of that office have done in the past years you can clearly demonstrate a thimble filled with nothing by the greater majority of them. This is no different in the Lodge where the average Master is about 2.5 to 3 year a Master Mason with very little if any preparation for what he is about to engage in.

If you look at their accomplishments as to how much money they have collected for a particular project, I will tell you that it is not based on him, but on many other factors such as the economy, who they have in charge of it at the local level, how much they beg of the Lodges and sometimes how much money they ask to be given to one project over another for the benefit of their program. I have seen all the tricks and some Grand Masters have cheapened the Office by the quick pro quo deals they have agreed to in order to raise more funds.

In case of the Lodges you will find that very little fund raising is done. If any is done it is by very few Brothers. They keep the Lodge dues and Degree Fees so low that the Lodges are barely scraping by or find themselves and object of Charity from a few Brothers. This is really not the position any Lodge should find itself in. In most cases the Lodges do not have enough funds to help a Brother in need. Although more times than I care to admit they give to a stranger over a Brother, mostly for two reasons they do not have sufficient funds or they are not that well in touch with their membership to know who is in need.

This says much about small Lodges where the Brothers are better acquainted with each other and share a stronger bond of Brotherhood because they have more time to get to know each other and socialize. Sideliners will notice those Brothers missing from their midst and look into the reasons why they are not present. This communicates to the Brother that he is missed. Additionally, this will give the Lodge Officers an opportunity to look into the Brothers reported and missed, making the Lodge a stronger Fraternity and allow them to stay in touch with their core membership, if they are truly going to serve them properly.

Although everyone in the Masonic structure, at whatever level, needs to remember their obligations and charges of every Degree and those of the swearing in ceremonies of their responsibilities as it relates to their newly elected and installed station in the Institution, the majority of those taking their obligations are so accustomed to hearing the words being said that they hear them as mere formalities. No one pays attention to them. "Don't worry about it" is the attitude of many.

This is the reality of Freemasonry today. In many

Jurisdictions we have not guarded our West Gate well and much worse we have done nothing to make a difference in those individuals' characters. As a result, many of them have reached leadership status over the years and will continue in the future. We have not taken care of business; we are not Making Good Men Better.

Here is another thing, that although at one point it was a great achievement and an act of compassion, today it has become a burden in many of the Jurisdictions and that is their nursing homes. Some states are doing very well where a larger percentage have not done so well and have closed them. In many of the states they have introduced non-Masons into their nursing homes as a way of keeping their doors open, and it has worked. In others it has become a greater problem and is failing. The ones that are left that do not have them set up to accept non-Masons are struggling and they seem to consume or at least be the excuse for the Grand Lodge Officers to ignore the Fraternal side. Usually the attention goes where the money is and the endowment funds or trust of the nursing homes are so much larger than that of the Grand Lodges that the tail wags the dog.

The Grand Lodges Officers need to reassign more time to spend on the Fraternity. I can assure you that if the Fraternity does well everything else falls into place. If the Fraternity is not doing well, everything else starts to dwindle from participations to donations. Well informed and knowledgeable Masons never abandon their obligations or responsibilities.

We need to remain at the local level making an impact on the neediest that have fallen through the cracks and our very own that are often ignored.

We need to slow down the race to becoming a Worshipful

Master, District Deputy, District Instructor/Lecturer and Grand Lodge Officer by selecting these Brothers for multiple years. This will allow the Brothers serving more time to learn about our Fraternity and attend to its needs in real time, if not remove them.

We need to expect that those in charge will be forceful in expecting nothing but excellence from those that serve with him as his representatives, in whatever position. If they do not perform their duties, it should be brought to their attentions and a warning given. If they continue with their poor or no performance they should be stripped of their title and replaced with someone competent, irrespective of how many times someone has to be appointed, until the right Brother can be found.

If by now you are thinking hold on we are volunteers, let me remind you of what a volunteer is. A Volunteer is someone who enters into, or offers himself for, any service of his own free will, especially when done without pay. Like the Volunteer Fireman or Rescue personnel who donate their time, commits to service, and dedicate themselves to the cause of helping others. Nowhere in the definition of a Volunteer did it say when I had time, when or if I wanted to do it. It always speaks of commitment, dedication and sacrifice to help or do something for no compensation.

The reality is that all too often too many Brothers are appointed to perform certain duties and they fail the person who appointed them and those he was supposed to serve, and nothing is done to them for their failure to live up to their commitments and responsibilities. Most of the time these Brothers get promoted to the next place or station, committee or chairmanship. Some of these Brothers have had impressive accumulations of titles with the exception of Grand Architect of The Universe, although some of them think they deserve that too, or at least act like they are it.

When electing or recommending a Brother to an Office we must be certain that we look at the Brother in detail and scrutinize everything he does and says and make sure we bring it up to their attention by whispering wise counsel when they deviate from what they promised. Further, do not go by their resume of committees and positions they have held, but instead look at the Proceeding of your Grand Lodge to see if they really performed their duties, although I'm sure that by that time they would have learned enough to pass the buck and blame it on someone else. You should ask them to validate their credentials. You may say that I'm going too far, and I will say, when it comes to the future of our beloved Fraternity it is never too far. The same can be said of the Lodges, although they have no proceedings. If you are a regular attendant you will know who has completed their assignments and who has not. There is no place in Lodge or in life for Social Promotions lest we decide to throw our future to luck instead of proven hard work.

Guarding the West Gate has become increasingly harder. Our mentality and drive for membership at whatever cost has made taboo the rejection of an unqualified candidate. Today everyone gets alarmed when a candidate is rejected, and we take the side of an unknown individual over the objection of a Brother who has been a steadfast member of the Fraternity. This is one of those paradoxes that I cannot understand but continue to look at the reasons for this behavior.

We forget that even our ritual warns us of how weak we are as an Institution when it comes to allowing new members in and that we must be careful of the material we recommend and who we allow to join our Fraternity.

As discussed in earlier chapters about the Recommenders and the Investigation Committee, the reason we have these steps before allowing someone to join is because we were allowing indiscriminate access to our Fraternity and it was killing the values. Therefore, we created a central government that would hold the same standards in all the Lodges.

Our predecessors of long ago realized that we could not depend on all of the recommenders to bring the absolute best material to present to the Lodge for membership. They understood that these individuals would be biased towards their family and friends, and they also understood the general trust Brothers would place on the recommenders as their Brothers not to violate their obligations and to do the absolute right thing by the Fraternity not to recommend undesirables. However, we know that this is not true and that the Fraternity has discovered many candidates where we have national background investigations including men wanted for murder, who had been recommended to the Lodge by well-intended Brothers that are looking to increase our numbers while disregarding the fact that they truly did not know the individual who was being recommended.

This is why we have an additional step, which is called the Investigation Committee. Now, in some cases they are handpicked by those in charge because they know they will not perform their duties and allow anyone to go through regardless of how shady their past may have been. They have either forgotten their obligations or their responsibilities to the Craft or again taken them as mere words since no one has been held accountable for their failure to perform the duties entrusted to them on behalf of the Craft for its own wellbeing.

One thing I can tell you is if they would be legally

liable for any funds or violations made by the individual they recommended, they would think twice before they so liberally placed their names on the petitions. Shame on them, because I personally take my word to be worth more than any material assets I may have.

We have placed so little value on our Institution that we have kept our fees for Degrees and our Dues so low on average that when I reviewed the dues in my state nearly 37% of our Lodge's dues were less than fifteen cents a day, 18% less than twenty cents a day, and 18% less than twenty-five cents a day. When looking at the Degree Fees the total cost of them is set by the regulation to be at a minimum of $100.00 for all three Degrees and the majority of the Lodges have kept them that low. The excuses are that the young people are strung out with so many burdens that they cannot afford anything more. This just blows my mind; as if generations before them had everything they wanted or needed all of their lives.

This of course flies in the face of the truth because these are the same young people that have at least a phone that is worth between $300 to $600 dollars with a monthly bill of several hundred dollars with all the bells and whistles. This is the same person who pays a couple of hundred dollars for tennis shoes, drinks $5.00 cups of coffee, belongs to clubs that cost him several hundred dollars a year and the list goes on. They themselves have claimed in many surveys that we are too cheap to be able to deliver on what we promise, and I agree we are too cheap but that is not the reason we cannot deliver on our promise. The real reason is that we don't have that many people who can deliver on the promise, but this too can change if we elect and appoint the right Mason in positions of authority. We need to get back to basics.

Start charging what the Fraternity is worth both in Dues

and Degree Fees, and deliver the product we committed ourselves to deliver when we promised we would "Make Good Men Better."

So where do we go from here? As I see it we need to look at all the items discussed in this book and if you agree you make them your cause. You stand for principles. Teach those around you. Build consensus within your Fraternal circles if our leadership is not going to take the helm and lead on these core principles and make the changes needed. We must create a grass roots movement that would challenge the Brothers seeking to represent us to act on them. If they do not support them do not vote for them. Sooner or later someone will come along whether it comes from the movement or supports the movement's ideals and principles which must at all times be those of Freemasonry. If our leadership is not going to lead we must elect Brothers that will.

Stimulate Brothers to become well versed with the Constitutions, Rules, Regulations and Edicts of your Jurisdiction, By-laws of their Lodges, Usages and Customs of your Jurisdiction, Ancient Charges, Masonic Etiquette, and any educational material your Jurisdiction may offer. Together with any information relating to Masonry, it's imperative that you are well informed. You cannot lead if you do not have the light necessary to illuminate the path of those seeking knowledge.

Our key to success is to use the Liberal Sciences in order to understand our places and the demands placed on us by our Fraternity as practicing Masons. Reading and research will be required in order to be successful. Are you up to par with these requirements? If not you will only be fooling yourself. My Brothers, an Educated Mason is a Dedicated Mason and as such he too will be a well-rounded leader and member of the

Craft, understanding our needs and stepping up to the plate for the sake of our beloved Fraternity to make our promise a reality of "Making Good Men Better." You are the key to Freemasonry's success. Here I leave you with M.W. Dwight L. Smith thoughts after a long look at our Fraternity's problems where he was convinced that the solution to "Freemasonry's problem is Freemasonry." Why don't we try it?

God Bless you and our Fraternity, wheresoever dispersed.

Made in the USA
San Bernardino, CA
14 March 2018